D0344552

AN INSTANT GUIDE TO

REPTILES
& AMPHIBIANS

The most familiar species of
North American reptiles and amphibians
described and illustrated in full color

Pamela Forey and Cecilia Fitzsimons

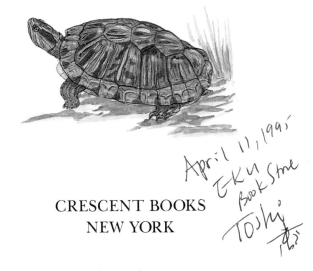

CRESCENT BOOKS
NEW YORK

April 11, 1995
EKu Stone
Book Store
Toshy

WARNING

Throughout this book the following symbols have been used to denote aggressive, toxic or dangerous animals:

 Aggressive or **toxic**   **Dangerous**

Readers are advised to treat all reptiles and amphibians with caution.
If in doubt, keep your distance!

Aggressive. Will attack or defend themselves by biting (a bite may vary from a painful nip to a severe laceration) or scratching with sharp claws or both.
Toxic. Skin secretions of toads are irritating to the skin of anyone handling them especially to eyes, mouth and nose and may cause serious injury or death to dogs.
Dangerous. Venom produced by snakes carrying the danger symbol is deadly and their bite requires immediate first aid and subsequent medical treatment. The Alligator and Gila Monster are also dangerous.

This 1987 edition published by Crescent Books, distributed by Outlet Book Company, Inc., a Random House Company, 225 Park Avenue South, New York, New York 10003.

Manufactured in Singapore

ISBN 0-517-61800-1

8 7 6 5 4 3

CONTENTS

Introduction

This is a book for those people who, although they may know little of the amphibians and reptiles of North America, are interested in them and would like to know more, but do not have the time or opportunity to make a close study of them. Most amphibians and reptiles are elusive animals, more often glimpsed than seen clearly and often living in wilderness areas. Some however, like some of the lizards, are seen more frequently, on roadsides, fences or rocks; others, like some of the frogs, are more often heard than seen. Most are harmless and afraid of man, but some turtles, lizards and snakes are aggressive and other snakes are highly dangerous.

This book describes about 140 of the most common species of amphibians and reptiles found in the USA and Canada. Its chief aim is to enable the reader, and newcomer to the study of these animals, to identify positively and as simply as possible, any of them which he is likely to encounter. Those that are aggressive, toxic, dangerous or venomous are clearly indicated as such (although they are in the minority), so that they can be avoided.

How to use this book

There are two quite different groups of animals described in this book, **Amphibians** and **Reptiles**. They are divided into seven sections, two of Amphibians: **Salamanders**; **Frogs and Toads**: and five of Reptiles: **Turtles**; **Crocodiles and Alligators**; **Lizards**; **Harmless Snakes**; and **Venomous Snakes**. Each section is indicated by a different color band at the top of the page (see Contents page). To identify your animal, first decide whether it is an Amphibian or Reptile and then to which section it belongs, using the information and symbols in the *Guide to Identification* which follows.

Guide to identification

First decide whether your animal is an Amphibian or a Reptile. This is not difficult since they have quite different skin. Amphibians have soft moist skins with no scales, most have smooth skin although the skin of toads may be rough and warty. There are no claws on their toes. Reptiles have hard, dry, scale-covered skin. Those that have limbs have sharp claws on the toes. However snakes and some lizards have no limbs. Page numbers given at the end of each section will also enable you to turn directly to the relevant section.

Amphibians

Salamanders Small wet-skinned amphibians with long bodies and long tails. Most of them have four legs, but some are legless or lack hind limbs. They live in water or wet places and are most often active at night. Their young may hatch directly from eggs or may begin life as tadpoles. Some mature without metamorphosing (a sudden change in form, usually accompanied by changes in lifestyle, feeding habits etc., i.e. tadpoles into frogs), while still looking like large tadpoles with external gills. Salamanders are sometimes mistaken for lizards, but lizards are reptiles with scaly skins and claws on their toes.

14–31

Frogs and Toads Small, moist amphibians with short bodies and no tails. They have long limbs, the hind limbs longer than the fore limbs. True frogs, treefrogs and narrow-mouthed toads have smooth wet skins, spadefoot toads have relatively smooth skins but with many warts while true toads have drier, rough, warty skins. Eggs of frogs and toads are deposited in water and develop into tadpoles which later metamorphose into adults.

True toads have large special glands behind the ear drums, called parotoid glands, which secrete a thick milky poisonous substance. This irritates and inflames the mouth and eyes and affects breathing and heartbeat; it deters predators. Dogs which attack toads rarely do so again and some may die.

32–51

Reptiles

Turtles Small to large reptiles with highly distinctive "shells," made up of a more or less domed section above called the carapace and a flat section on the underside called the plastron. The shell is made of many interlocking bony plates and in most turtles is covered with horny scutes (shield-like plates). The head, limbs and tail are covered with scales.

52–68

Crocodiles and Alligators Very large, dangerous, semi-aquatic reptiles with long bodies and large muscular tails, covered with armor-like plates. They have four well-developed limbs and the hind limbs are longer than the fore limbs.

69

Lizards   Small to moderately large reptiles with long bodies and tails, and usually with four well-developed limbs; a few lizards, however, have tiny weak legs or are limbless and snake-like in appearance. They have dry scale-covered skin and their toes are clawed (features which immediately distinguish them from salamanders which have a similar body shape but wet skin and no claws).   **70–88**

Snakes   Small to moderately large reptiles, with long, cylindrical, legless, scale-covered bodies, no eyelids on their eyes and no external ear openings. (Snake-like lizards have movable eyelids and external ear openings.) Some snakes have smooth scales and are consequently smooth in appearance, others have keeled scales (scales with longitudinal ridges) and are rough in appearance.

Harmless snakes   Most North American snakes are harmless (96 out of 115) and kill their prey by constriction. Their fangs mostly lack venom (the fangs of the Night Snake contain venom but it is not dangerous to man), although some of them are aggressive and can give a nasty bite if surprised or cornered.   **89–111**

Venomous snakes   Nineteen of the snake species in North America are dangerous to man. Of these, all but four are rattlesnakes, which can be identified by the rattles on their tails. Coral Snakes are brightly colored with a distinctive color pattern, but the Cottonmouth and Copperhead are more difficult to identify and any snake, suspected of being one of these two, should be avoided.   **112–121**

Habitat symbols

When you have decided to which section your amphibian or reptile belongs, you will find that each section is further subdivided by habitat — the place where the animal lives — indicated by the symbol at the top of the page. There are four major habitat divisions indicated by these symbols. They are designed to help you confirm your identification of an animal. If you are in a camp site, sitting beside a mountain stream, then you are only likely to see animals designated as living in the stream (those having the freshwater symbol), or those designated as living beside water on its banks; however, you will not see animals which live in dry habitats. Many of the animals do live in more than one of the habitat types, for instance frogs live both in and beside freshwater streams; some snakes live in a wide variety of habitats from damp bottomlands to dry mountain slopes.

Fig. 1 Key to habitats

 Seawater
Three of the turtles are ocean-going species and may be seen off the coasts.

 Freshwater
In rivers, streams, ponds, lakes, marshes, swamps, ditches, canals, seeps and springs.

 Wet Terrestrial
Beside and on the margins of ponds, lakes, streams, rivers and marshes; also in wet meadows and woods or in damp places like rotting logs or beneath stones.

 Dry Terrestrial
Deserts, flats, canyons, dry woods and prairie grassland, sagebrush, chaparral and pine barrens; on roadsides, fences, rocks and rocky ledges.

Making a positive identification

Once you have decided on the section to which your animal belongs, you can turn to the pages on which the individual species are described and illustrated. The size of the animal, from the tip of the head to the tip of the tail, is given in the colored band at the top of the page. Four boxes provide information which make positive identification possible. The first box provides details of features or combinations of features which, together with the illustration, enable you to identify your animal. The second box gives you supplementary information on the biology of your animal. Habitat and distribution are given in the third box and a distribution map is provided for quick reference. Finally, the fourth box indicates some of the species with which this amphibian or reptile might be confused.

Characteristic features

Included in this box is a general indication of the shape of the animal where relevant; its color and markings; and any other characteristic features, like the shape of the "spade" in spadefoot toads, the texture of the scales in snakes or the shape of the carapace in turtles.

Biology of the animal

Included here is the time of day at which this particular species is most likely to be seen, together with any hiding places in which it may be found. The nature of the animal, whether it is peaceful or aggressive, dangerous or venomous is also described, together with its reaction to disturbance. If it is aggressive, toxic or dangerous, a symbol to indicate this has been included in the illustration.

Aggressive or toxic   **Dangerous**

An attempt has been made to indicate the distinctive sound made by each frog, although this is always difficult to do. Feeding habits are also given. For amphibians, some information on their eggs is also included, since these are as likely to be found as the adults. Turtles' egg-laying habits have also been given since many turtles only appear on land when laying eggs.

Habitat and distribution
There is wide variation in climate and geography in North America, from the mountains and tundra of the far north, to the deserts of the southwest and the rivers of the southeast. The area and habitats in which amphibians and reptiles are found often provide important clues to their identity. Amphibians are generally found in wet places or in water (exceptions being some of the toads which may burrow or hide beneath rocks in prairies or deserts). They are most common in the wetter east and west, and are much less common in the drier central areas of the continent. Turtles, being mostly water dwellers, also follow this pattern of distribution. Lizards and snakes, however, are generally found in drier areas and the greatest number of them live in the southwest.

The distribution map will help you to see at a glance whether any particular amphibian or reptile occurs in your part of North America. The third box on each page provides additional information about habitat and distribution, since an animal may not be common, or even present throughout the whole of its range, being confined to those areas within the range with a suitable habitat.

Fig. 2 Distribution map

● Common in this area, within its habitat limitations

○ Partial distribution only or reaching the limits of its distribution in this area

Similar species
In the fourth box are given some of the similar animals with which this one might be confused. Those similar species printed in **heavy type** are illustrated, either as featured animals or in the pages of *Other common species*, those in ordinary type are not illustrated. Not all related or similar species have been mentioned, since there are many amphibians

and reptiles in North America which are confined to one relatively small area. Many of the less common snakes and lizards of the southwest have been omitted as have the rarer frogs, salamanders and turtles from the southeast. Many snake species are highly variable and in these cases the fourth box has been used to indicate some of the color types found within the species.

Other common species
At the end of most of the sections you will find pages of other common species. These are less widespread than the featured species or less likely to be encountered. A brief description of each is given, together with some details of its habitat and distribution.

Fig. 3 Specimen page

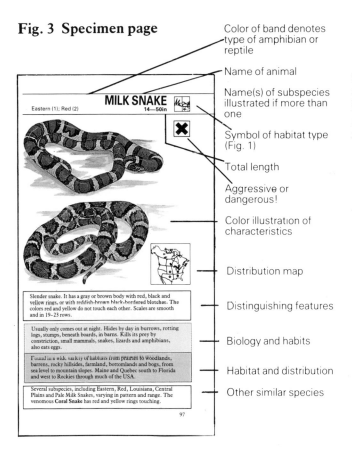

Color of band denotes type of amphibian or reptile

Name of animal

Name(s) of subspecies illustrated if more than one

Symbol of habitat type (Fig. 1)

Total length

Aggressive or dangerous!

Color illustration of characteristics

Distribution map

Distinguishing features

Biology and habits

Habitat and distribution

Other similar species

MILK SNAKE
Eastern (1); Red (2)
14—50in

Slender snake. It has a gray or brown body with red, black and yellow rings, or with reddish-brown black-bordered blotches. The colors red and yellow do not touch each other. Scales are smooth and in 19–23 rows.

Usually only comes out at night. Hides by day in burrows, rotting logs, stumps, beneath boards, in barns. Kills its prey by constriction, small mammals, snakes, lizards and amphibians, also eats eggs.

Found in a wide variety of habitats from prairies to woodlands, barrens, rocky hillsides, farmland, bottomlands and bogs, from sea level to mountain slopes. Maine and Quebec south to Florida and west to Rockies through much of the USA.

Several subspecies, including Eastern, Red, Louisiana, Central Plains and Pale Milk Snakes, varying in pattern and range. The venomous **Coral Snake** has red and yellow rings touching.

97

HELLBENDER
12—20in

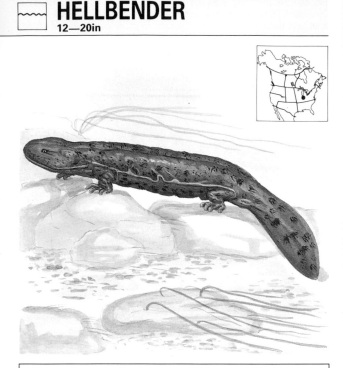

A large, slimy, aquatic salamander with loose, wrinkled skin and prominent folds on sides. Head and body horizontally flattened. Olive-brown or gray with darker spots.

May be caught by fishermen. Not poisonous as widely believed. Feeds on crayfish, worms, insect larvae and small fishes. Eggs deposited by female in fall, in tangled strands in saucer-shaped nest made by male beneath submerged rock or log.

Lives under stones or logs in clear, fast-flowing rocky rivers and streams at less than 2500ft. New York State to Alabama and Georgia, Susquehanna and Mississippi river systems, tributaries of Ohio, Tennessee, Black and Missouri rivers.

Ozark Hellbender: dark conspicuous blotches on back and lower lips, found in Black River system in Missouri and Arkansas.

MUDPUPPY
8—13in

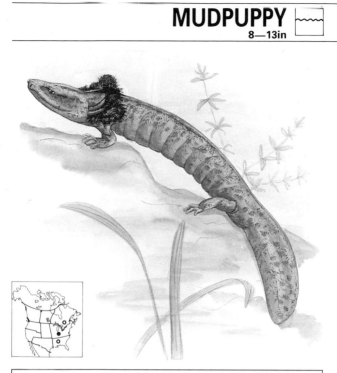

Dark olive-brown or gray aquatic salamander with a pale dark-spotted underside. It has four short stout legs with four toes on each foot. There are three pairs of dark red, feathery, external gills just behind the head, even in adults.

Mostly nocturnal, except in very muddy water where it may be active by day. Feeds on crayfish, mollusks, worms and aquatic insects. Eggs laid singly on the undersides of submerged stones and logs in early summer. May be caught by fishermen.

Lives in muddy or weedy waters of lakes, ponds, streams and rivers. Southern Quebec to Manitoba, northeastern USA and south to Louisiana and Oklahoma, to the Missouri and Tennessee river systems.

Waterdogs are very similar southern USA salamanders but are smaller, up to nine or ten inches long.

15

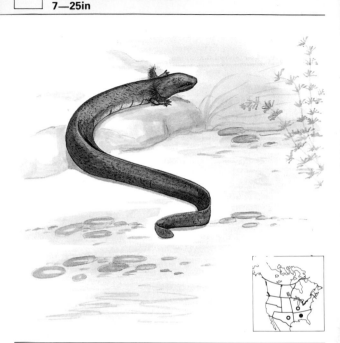

An eel-like salamander with small front legs and no hind legs. Three pairs of bluish external gills are present just behind the head. Dark gray or brown with scattered spots.

These salamanders can survive if the pond dries out, for they remain buried in the mud and survive in a cocoon even in baked mud. Eggs laid in sheltered hole in water in winter or spring. Feeds on crayfish, worms and mollusks, also on water plants.

Hides by day under stones, logs, in tangled water plants or in debris at the bottom of still warm ponds, ditches and swamps. Coastal plain from South Carolina to Florida and Texas, also in the Mississippi river valley as far north as Michigan.

Greater Siren: may be difficult to distinguish but is generally larger, found in southeastern USA in coastal plain. **Amphiumas** have four legs and no external gills.

THREE-TOED AMPHIUMA

20—30in

An eel-like aquatic salamander with four tiny limbs. Each limb has three toes. Dark brown to black on back, much lighter on underside. Can give severe bite.

These salamanders may be caught by fishermen who call them "congo eels" or "ditch eels." They feed on crayfish, frogs and small fishes. Eggs laid in single strand in water in summer.

Usually hides in tangle of vegetation or pile of debris with head protruding, in marshes, lakes, cypress swamps, ditches or slow-moving streams. From Alabama to Texas and in Mississippi river valley as far north as Missouri and Kentucky.

Two-toed Amphiuma is dark all over, has only two toes on each limb. **Sirens** have external gills and no hind limbs.

Mostly aquatic, a small stout animal with fore limbs smaller than hind limbs and a knife-edged flattened tail. Variable in color and markings. Usually gray or brown with a light line from the angle of the jaw to the eye. Underside speckled.

Mostly nocturnal. Feeds on worms, insects and insect larvae. Eggs laid in summer in grape-like clusters beneath submerged rocks or logs.

Lives in springs, seeps and small woodland brooks, especially where stones and debris provide cover. Eastern USA from New England to Louisiana but not in southeastern coastal plain or northwest of Ohio or Indiana.

Similar Dusky Salamanders best recognized by range. Southern Dusky Salamander lives in southeastern coastal plain. Mountain Dusky Salamander, near mountain seeps, New York to Georgia.

RED SALAMANDER

A semi-aquatic salamander, bright red with many irregular black spots when young, darkening to purple-brown with age and becoming mottled rather than spotted. Legs and tail both short.

Hides under logs or stones, or in crevices. Feeds on aquatic insect larvae, snails and crustaceans. Eggs laid in fall in jelly attached in masses to undersides of submerged stones.

Found in water of cool springs and brooks, especially where the bottom is rocky or gravelly. Mostly east of Mississippi River, from New York state and Indiana south to Mississippi and into Louisiana. Absent from southeastern coastal plain.

Spring Salamander: mountain springs of eastern USA. **Mud Salamander:** muddy streams and ponds of southeastern coastal plain and piedmont. **Red eft** of **Newt** is terrestrial.

19

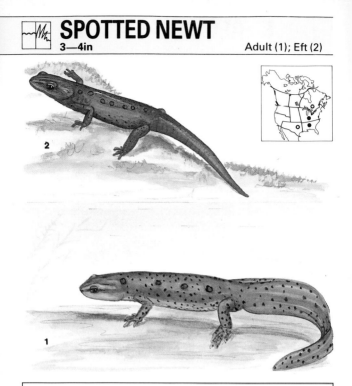

Adults are aquatic and smooth-skinned with tails compressed from side to side; yellow-brown or green in color with black spots and often with red spots. Efts are orange-red with rough warty skins and rounded tails.

Females lay eggs on water plants in spring. Young leave water as subadults or efts in fall and live on land for up to three years. When mature they return to water. Adults can be kept in aquaria. Feed on insects, worms, frogs' eggs and mollusks.

Adults live in ponds, lakes, swamps and ditches where water plants grow thickly. Efts live under logs and stones in woodland. Eastern USA and Canada from Nova Scotia to Great Lakes, south to Florida and Texas.

Mud and **Red Salamanders** are red aquatic salamanders. Other adult newts lack the red spots, some have broken red or yellow stripes; none are so widely distributed as this species.

20

TWO-LINED SALAMANDER

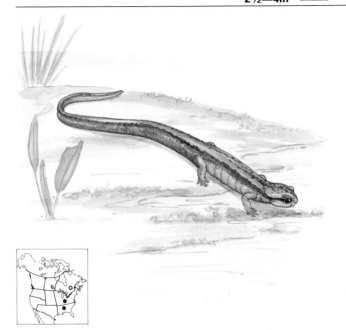

2½—4in

A semi-aquatic salamander with a long tail. It has a broad yellow stripe on its back, bordered with a dark brown or black line on each side. Tail flattened from side to side.

Although normally found in water, in wet weather this salamander may be found in more terrestrial habitats like woodland. Feeds on aquatic insects and snails. Eggs laid in small clusters on undersides of submerged logs and rocks.

Lives in brooks and streams, or on their edges, in seeps, moist soil, under logs and stones in wet places, from the coast to mountain areas. Quebec south to northern Florida and Mississippi, east of Great Lakes and Mississippi River.

Long-tailed Salamander: yellowish all over with small black spots. Similar Dusky Salamanders have a light line between the eye and the angle of the jaw.

FOUR-TOED SALAMANDER
2—4in

A small semi-terrestrial salamander with four toes on the hind feet (most eastern salamanders have five toes on hind feet), and a constriction at the base of the long tail. Reddish-brown with gray sides and white black-spotted underside.

Nocturnal. Adults gather near sphagnum pools in spring and females lay eggs in moss. They then protect the eggs by curling around them until they hatch. Young make their way into the water.

Found in sphagnum bogs and swamps, especially in woodland areas for much of the year, hiding under logs or stones or in moss. Nova Scotia to Wisconsin and south to Louisiana, but more local in south.

No other species with the same appearance and life style.

PACIFIC GIANT SALAMANDER

7—10in

A semi-aquatic salamander, thick-bodied with a large head and stout limbs. Gray or purple-brown in color on the back and marbled with black, with light yellow-brown underside.

Makes a noise like a small dog barking. Feeds on insects and tadpoles, small rodents and garter snakes. Eggs laid singly in spring in headwaters of streams; larvae develop for up to two years, growing to six inches long, before they metamorphose.

Lives in streams or in moist places nearby, under logs and stones in cool humid forest areas; may climb into shrubs and trees. Southwest B.C. along coast and Cascade mountains to California. Also in Rocky Mountains in Idaho and Montana.

Large size and marbled color on back are not found in any other western salamander.

ENSATINA
3—5in

Monterey (1); Yellow-blotched (2)

Terrestrial. Only western salamander with five toes on hind feet and a constriction at base of tail. Color very variable, brown or black, some forms with spots, blotches or mottled effect in yellow or orange; others plain. Underside whitish.

Lives in damp places, under logs or bark and stones, or in rodent burrows. Feeds on spiders and insects. Eggs laid in late spring underground and guarded by female, young hatch in fall and immediately adopt terrestrial life-style.

Lives in chaparral-live oak woods and redwood forests along Pacific coast, yellow pine-black oak woods in Sierra Nevada, Douglas fir-maple forests in northwest. From Vancouver island and southern B.C. along coast and western mountains to Calif.

Long-toed Salamander: may be superficially similar to yellow-blotched form but has no constriction at base of tail and has four toes on hind feet.

24

CALIF. SLENDER SALAMANDER
3—6in

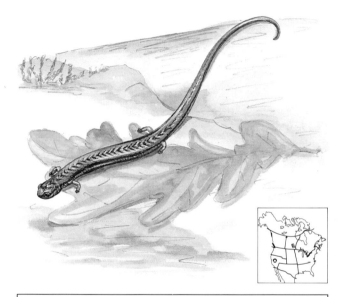

A slender terrestrial salamander with a long tail. It has four toes on each of the four narrow feet. Dark gray or black with a broad reddish stripe on its back and a dark white-speckled underside.

Feeds on spiders and insects. Eggs laid in fall and winter in cavities beneath rocks or logs. Young hatch in spring and immediately adopt terrestrial life-style.

Lives in moist leaf litter, in rodent burrows or in rotting wood in redwood and live oak forests in the mountains and coastal forests of California.

Other Slender Salamanders live in the west but are restricted in their habitats and ranges. They include the Garden Slender Salamander from Calif. and the Oregon Slender Salamander.

SPOTTED SALAMANDER
6—8in

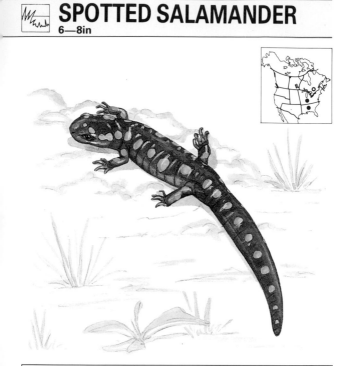

A terrestrial burrowing salamander. Thick-bodied, with a broad head and four stout limbs. Black or slate-colored with two rows of bright yellow, round spots along the whole length of the back. Underside slate gray.

These salamanders come out at night to feed on worms, insects and mollusks. They congregate on spring nights at woodland ponds to lay their eggs in compact masses of jelly, attached to water plants or submerged branches. Often kept in terraria.

Most of the year is spent in abandoned burrows (of moles and other mammals), or under logs or stones, usually in mixed hardwood and deciduous forests. Nova Scotia to Ontario, south to Georgia and Texas, as far west as Wisconsin in USA.

Long-toed Salamander: yellow marks in single irregular stripe, not in double row of spots; northwestern USA and Canada.

26

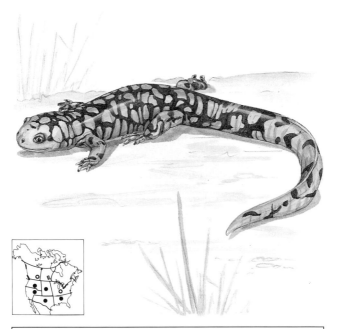

The largest terrestrial salamander. A thick-bodied animal with a broad head and four stout limbs. Very variable in color, black or brown with extensive lighter yellow or green spots, blotches or stripes; underside yellowish.

Migrate in wet weather (in winter in south, late summer in southwest, spring in north) to ponds to spawn. Most likely to be seen on wet nights. Some western forms mature without metamorphosing (axolotls) and spend their lives in water.

Lives for most of the year in burrows, under stones or logs in damp places in forests, barrens, prairies or mountains. Southern Canada from B.C. to Saskatchewan and in much of USA but rare in Appalachians, northeast and Pacific states.

Long-toed Salamander: dark brown with irregular yellow stripe along the length of the back. Ringed Salamander: body brown with circular yellow stripes, Ozarks and Ouachita Mountains.

MARBLED SALAMANDER
3—5in

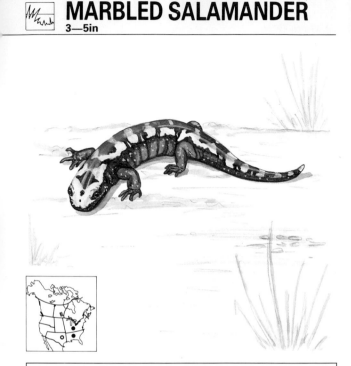

A terrestrial salamander. Thick-bodied with a broad head and four stout limbs. Black with variable silvery cross-bands, sometimes complete or running together, sometimes more like spots. Underside black.

In the fall females lay their eggs near water and guard them till they hatch. The young make their way into the water, emerging in spring to adopt the terrestrial life-style of the adults. Feeds on worms, insect grubs and mollusks.

Lives in woodland and other shady habitats, under stones or logs in quite dry areas for much of the year. Eastern USA, from New England to northern Florida and west to Illinois, Missouri and Texas.

Ringed Salamander: brown body with circular yellow, not silvery, stripes; found in Ozarks and Ouachita mountains.

REDBACKED SALAMANDER
Red-backed (1); Lead-backed (2)   2—3½in

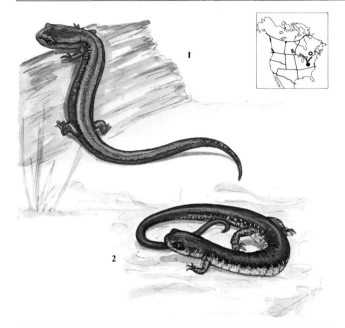

A small slender terrestrial salamander with four legs. Two color phases: red-backed form has broad red stripe on back and a gray body, lead-backed form is uniformly dark gray. In both forms the underside is mottled black and white.

Active at night in leaf litter, searching for insects and worms. Female lays grape-like cluster of eggs in moist cavity in rotting wood in June or July and curls around them. Young hatch and take up terrestrial life, after about two months.

Lives in moist coniferous forests, hiding by day in stumps, under rotting logs or in woodland debris. Newfoundland to southern Ontario, Great Lakes region, south to North Carolina and Indiana.

Several related salamanders, none have the mottled underside. Zigzag Salamander has wavy reddish stripe on back, found in rocky ravines, caves and seeps from Indiana to Oklahoma.

EASTERN SALAMANDERS

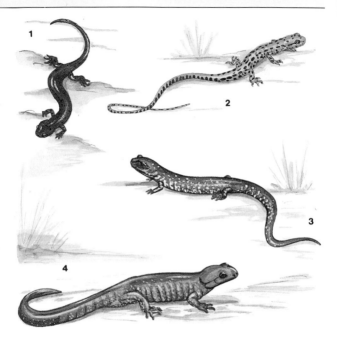

Mud Salamander (1)
Stout salamander with short tail
& short legs. Coral-pink or red
with scattered, round black
spots. Bottom of muddy ponds
& streams, in coastal plain &
piedmont from New Jersey to
Florida, also west of
Appalachians.

Long-tailed Salamander (2)
Yellowish salamander with many
small black spots & a long tail
with dark vertical stripes on the
sides. Hides under logs or stones
near streams or in crevices. New
York south & west to northern
Florida and Missouri.

Slimy Salamander (3)
Black salamander with white or
yellowish spots on back & sides.
Skin exudes very slimy
substance which sticks to
fingers. Woodland areas, under
rocks or logs, in crevices,
ravines. New York to Florida &
west to Mississippi & Missouri.

Jefferson's Salamander (4)
A dark gray or brownish
salamander with long legs, hind
legs longer than fore legs, & long
toes. Lives under debris or near
swamps in deciduous woodland.
From New York state to
Indiana.

WESTERN SALAMANDERS

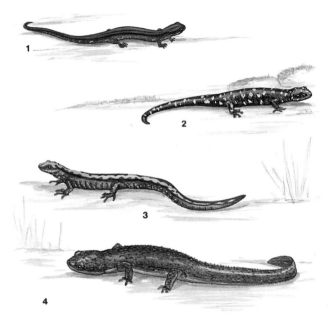

Western Red-backed Salamander (1) Similar to eastern Red-backed Salamander, with brownish stripe on back extending to tip of tail. Damp places, in bark of trees, under stones or logs in forests of southern B.C., Vancouver Island, Washington state & Oregon.

Black Salamander (2) Slender black salamander; many forms with whitish spots, others plain black or suffused with olive-green. Along stream margins, amongst moss-covered rocks & debris, in open forest areas of northern Calif.

Long-toed Salamander (3) Dark brown or black salamander with a variable yellow back stripe, irregular in outline or broken into blotches. Has long narrow toes. Under stones or logs in forests, mountain meadows & sagebrush, near water in early spring to spawn. Alaska through B.C. & Alberta to northern Calif.

Rough-skinned Newt (4) A dark brown, rough-skinned salamander with red underside. Lives near streams & ponds in forest & grassland areas along the Pacific coast, from southern Alaska to mid Calif.

LEOPARD FROG
2—5in

A slender frog with a narrow head. Green or brown with conspicuous ridges along each side of the back and two rows of rounded light-edged spots running between them; other spots on the sides.

Mostly nocturnal. Seen throughout the year in south, from early spring to fall in north. Feeds on insects. Eggs laid in jelly in water in spring. Voice: a low snore, followed by two or three "clucks."

Lives in all kinds of freshwater and brackish habitats, and in other damp shady places in summer when the vegetation is high. Southern Canada from eastern B.C. to Nova Scotia, south through much of the USA, east of the Rockies.

May be more than one Leopard Frog. Southern Leopard Frog lives in the east, Northern Leopard Frog in Canada and northern USA. **Pickerel Frog:** rows of squares on back and yellow underside.

Light brown frog with parallel rows of dark squares running along the length of its back. Underside and inside of hind legs yellow or orange. Secretes irritating substance from skin which makes this frog distasteful to predators.

Nocturnal. Emerges from hibernation in spring and eggs laid in masses of jelly in water in May. Feeds on worms, snails and insects. Voice: a low croak, males sometimes croak fully submerged.

Lives in or near cool clear ponds and bogs with dense water plants, and in wet grassy meadows. Southeastern Canada, south to the Carolinas and Texas but absent from southeastern corner of USA.

Leopard Frogs have rounded spots with light edges and no yellow inside to the hind limbs.

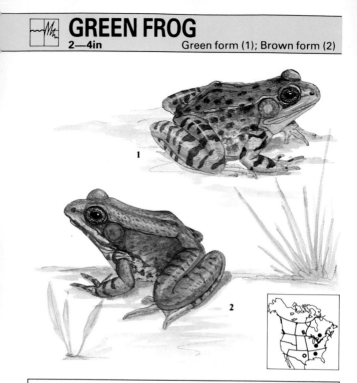

Green or brown in color, with white spotted underside. There is an obvious ridge on each side of the back that does not extend as far as the groin. Male has large external ear drum and yellow throat.

Mostly nocturnal. Feeds on aquatic insects and on insects that fly near water surface. Emerges from hibernation in the mud, in March. Eggs laid in masses of jelly in the water. Tadpoles metamorphose after two years. Voice: like a banjo string.

Lives in and beside streams, swamps, ponds and springs from southeastern Canada to Florida, west as far as Ontario and Texas.

Bullfrog is larger and has no ridges on the sides of its back. Pig Frog also has no ridges on its back, lives in marshes and ponds in southeastern USA.

34

BULLFROG

5—8in

The largest N. American frog. Green or brown, often with dark spots, and a white, often mottled, underside. It has no ridges on the sides of its back. Hind feet webbed but longest toe protrudes beyond webbing. Male has large external ear drum.

Nocturnal. Feeds on tadpoles, crayfish, mice, salamanders and worms. Emerges from hibernation in mud, in May. Eggs laid in masses of jelly in water. Tadpoles large, metamorphose in two years. Voice: a hoarse "jug-o-rum, more-rum."

Lives in and on the banks of large ponds, lakes and rivers throughout eastern USA; also in southeastern Canada and introduced in many places in western USA.

Green Frog is smaller and has ridges on each side of its back. Pig Frog: fourth toe of webbed hind foot extends only slightly beyond webbing, marshes and ponds of southeastern USA.

35

SPRING PEEPER
¾—1½in

A brown, gray or olive-green treefrog with a dark X-shaped mark on its back, often an incomplete one.

Nocturnal. Frogs "sing" from tussocks or bushes standing in water. Voice like high-pitched whistle of several notes, rising at end; chorus sounds like small bells. Hibernate in leaves or under bark. Eggs laid with warm rains in spring.

Found in woodland ponds, often in temporary ones, in brush and second growth woods, and swamps. The only treefrog found in Canada (from Manitoba eastwards) and northeastern USA, but also found throughout eastern USA except peninsular Florida.

Chorus Frogs overlap in range: they have no X-shaped mark on the back and most have a light line on upper lip.

36

CHORUS FROG

¾—1½in

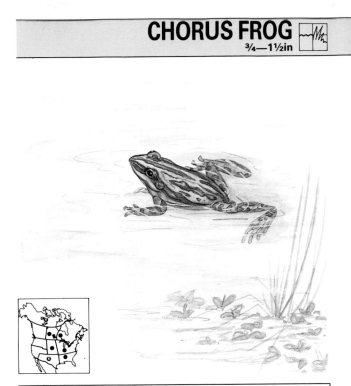

Gray-green or brown frog with three dark, often broken, stripes down its back, a dark stripe through each eye and a whitish underside. Males have a single large, light yellowish vocal pouch.

Nocturnal. Found all year in southern areas, spring and summer in north. They "sing" in a rasping trill in shallow water from first warm wet weather of northern spring, in cool wet weather in the south. Feed on insects. Eggs laid in masses in water.

Live on grassy banks of ponds and rivers, swamps and woodland from northwest Canada, south along eastern slopes of Rockies to Arizona, east to the Atlantic. Absent from extreme south, southeast coastal plain and northeast USA and Canada.

Several other chorus frogs including Mountain Chorus Frog in the Appalachians, Southern Chorus Frog in the southeastern coastal plain. **Spring Peeper:** chorus more "trilled."

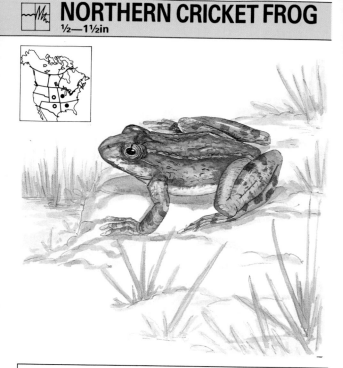

A rough-skinned frog, green and brown in color with a dark triangle between the eyes and one or more ragged longitudinal dark stripes on the backs of the thighs. Hind feet webbed.

Active by day, searching for spiders and insects. Eggs laid from April to July in masses of jelly in water. Voice: a series of clicks, getting faster.

Lives on edges of ponds and slow-moving streams with extensive water plants. Throughout eastern USA except Florida and extreme northeast, west as far as Texas and Nebraska.

Southern Cricket Frog: hind feet only partly webbed (first toe partly free of webbing and longest toe projects well beyond webbing), coastal plain of southeastern USA.

PACrIFIC TREEFROG

A rough-skinned treefrog, green or brown in color and often with darker spots. There is a dark stripe that extends from the nostril, through the eye, to the arm pit. Toes have toe pads and hind toes are webbed.

Mostly nocturnal. These frogs "sing" in chorus, with a two-note call, the second note higher than the first. Eggs laid in masses of jelly in shallow water, from January to May, depending on area.

Lives on the ground, in crevices, burrows and in vegetation on banks of streams and ponds from southern B.C. and Vancouver

Calif. Treefrog and Canyon Treefrog (found in Arizona and New Mexico) lack eye stripes.

39

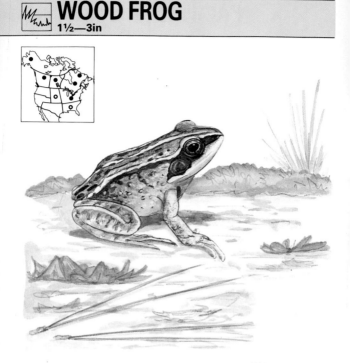

Pink, light brown or dark brown frog with a light underside.
There is a distinctive dark mask extending backwards behind each
eye and ending behind the ear drum, bordered below with a
narrow white stripe.

Terrestrial, hibernating in logs and under stones, returning to
ponds in spring before ice has melted, to spawn. Feeds on worms,
insects and snails. Eggs laid in masses of jelly in water. Can leap
four or five feet. Voice: a clucking sound.

Lives in moist woodland areas, or in grassland and tundra in west
and north. Northern North America from Alaska to
Newfoundland, south to the Canadian border and into eastern
USA to Wisconsin and south in the eastern mountains.

The Pacific **Red-legged Frog** has a similar mask, but its belly and
the insides of its legs are reddish. **Spotted Frog** has a less distinct
mask and is reddish or yellow on the underside.

40

CRAYFISH FROG

2—4in

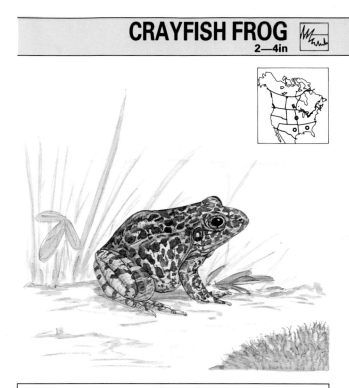

A stout, light brown to dark brown frog with many dark spots on its back and sides. Underside whitish. Ridges on back may have yellow highlights and skin on inside of hind legs may be yellow in males.

Nocturnal. Most likely to be seen at spawning pools in spring, usually after heavy rain. Feeds on a variety of prey, including other frogs. Eggs laid in masses of jelly in water. Voice: a loud resonant snore.

Hides by day in holes like those of Gopher Turtle or crayfishes, in lowland meadows, roadside banks and moist woods, near ponds. Red and Arkansas river valleys, coastal plain of southeast USA from Carolinas to Louisiana, north to Illinois.

Leopard Frogs appear more slender and have proportionately longer legs. **Pickerel Frog** has square spots.

GRAY TREEFROG
1¼—2½in

A gray-brown treefrog with warty skin and dark blotches on its back, changing color with background. It has a yellow-white spot beneath each eye and the insides of the thighs are bright orange-yellow. Highly effective sucking disks are on its toes.

Nocturnal. Descend to ground only in breeding season, in spring or summer, for rest of year they spend solitary lives in trees, clinging to bark with sucking disks. Feed on insects living in crevices of bark. Voice: a loud resonant trill.

Found high in trees and bushes growing in shallow standing water throughout much of eastern North America from southern Ontario to Florida and west to Minnesota and Texas.

Bird-voiced Treefrog: lives in swamps in southern USA, mostly in Louisiana and Mississippi; voice is a bird-like whistle.

Tailed Frog (1)
Olive-brown or gray frog, with many dark spots on back & a dark stripe across eye. "Tail" is copulatory organ in male. Mountain streams in forest areas from southern B.C. to Calif., also in northern Idaho & northwest Montana.

Spotted Frog (2)
Large brown frog, with dark spots & a yellow or red underside. Cold waters of streams, lakes, marshes & springs in Rockies from northern B.C. to Idaho & Montana; scattered in Washington, Oregon & Nevada.

Red-legged Frog (3)
Large brownish frog, with many dark spots. Underside yellow, tinged with red on belly & hind legs. Lives in damp vegetation & in woods near ponds from southern B.C. & Vancouver Island, south in Pacific states to Calif.

Green Treefrog (4)
A bright green, gray-green or yellow frog, with a distinct light stripe along side. Voice like a cowbell. Lives in wet places, in vegetation growing in the edges of ponds & marshes. Southeastern USA from New Jersey to Texas.

AMERICAN TOAD
2—3½in

A gray or brown toad with one or two large warts in the dark spots on its back. Underside white with dark spots. The large elongated parotoid glands are not connected with the bony crests behind the eyes.

Mostly nocturnal. Feeds on insects including flies, crickets and beetles, also on worms and slugs. Eggs laid in temporary pools of water, ponds, ditches or streams from March to July, in strings attached to vegetation. Voice: a musical trill.

Found in variety of habitats, from city gardens to mountains and woods, wherever there is water and insects to eat. Hides by day under stones, logs, boards or in burrows. Labrador to Manitoba in Canada and south in USA to Georgia and Oklahoma.

Woodhouse's Toad: parotoid gland connected with bony crest behind eye. **Southern Toad:** cranial crests form knobs in middle of head.

WOODHOUSE'S TOAD

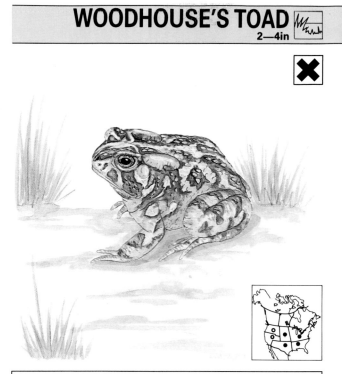

A greenish-gray, yellow or brownish toad, with three or more large warts in the dark spots on its back and a light stripe down the midline. Underside yellowish. The large parotoid glands are connected with the bony crests behind the eyes.

Mostly nocturnal. Feeds on insects, may be attracted to lights at night by the insects there. Eggs laid in strings attached to vegetation, in shallow water, cattle tanks, reservoirs, sloughs, between March and August. Voice: like bleating sheep.

Lives in burrow in loose soil or hidden in vegetation, in back yards, marshes, canyons, sandy lowland areas, lake and river margins throughout much of USA but absent from extreme southeast, Pacific and northern states.

American Toad: parotoid gland unconnected with bony crest behind eye; has many dark marks on chest. **Great Plains Toad:** cranial crests converge towards front of head.

WESTERN TOAD
2½—5in

Gray, greenish or brown in color, with many light-colored pitted warts and a light stripe down the center of the back. It has no bony crests behind the eyes and large oval parotoid glands.

Active in evening and night. Usually walks rather than hops. Feeds on insects. Eggs laid in strings attached to vegetation, in shallow water. Voice: like the peeping of a gosling—the call does not resonate since the toad has no vocal pouch.

Hides in burrows, under boards, stones or rocks by day, near water, in woods and meadows from the sea to the mountains. From Alaska south to Calif., through the Rocky Mountains and east to Alberta and Colorado.

Great Plains Toad, Canadian Toad, Woodhouse's Toad and Texas Toad all have cranial crests. Yosemite Toad lives in high Sierra Nevadas.

GREAT PLAINS TOAD
2—4½in

Gray, olive-brown or brown in color with large greenish blotches edged in white, on back and sides. Bony crests behind eyes converge towards the front of the head, and are connected to elongated parotoid glands.

Mostly nocturnal. Feeds on insects and insect grubs, like beetles and cutworms. Eggs laid in strings in pools, usually after heavy rain, between April and September. Voice: high-pitched vibrating trill.

Lives in shallow burrows in prairie and desert areas, in irrigation ditches, temporary pools and long grass areas from southern Alberta and the Dakotas south to northern Texas, New Mexico and Arizona.

Texas Toad has indistinct cranial crests; lives in dry grassland of Texas. **Woodhouse's Toad** has non-convergent cranial crests. **Western Toad** lacks cranial crests.

E. NARROW-MOUTHED TOAD
1—1½in

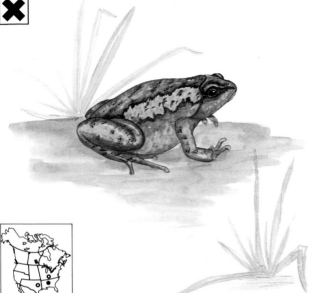

A small plump toad with a pointed head and a fold across the back of the head. Color varies from brown to gray, with varying numbers of spots and often mottled. Underside light in color, mottled with darker patches.

Mostly nocturnal and most likely to be encountered on wet rainy nights. Feeds on insects, particularly on ants. Eggs laid in small masses which float on the water, after heavy rain in summer. Voice: like the bleat of a lamb.

Spend most of their time in burrows, or sometimes found under logs, stones, in leaf litter or vegetation, on the borders of swamps and beside streams. From Virginia and the Carolinas, west to Oklahoma and south to Texas and Florida.

Great Plains Narrow-mouthed Toad: green-gray or gray-brown without mottling; found in moist woods or grasslands, often in burrows, from Kansas south to Texas.

48

A stout olive-brown toad, with two yellowish lines running the length of the back. Underside white or gray. On the inner side of each hind foot is a prominent sickle-shaped black tubercle, the spade, which is used for digging.

Nocturnal. Makes burrow by digging backwards into soft earth. Feeds on insects and worms. Eggs laid in bands of jelly in temporary pools, between March and September; tadpoles metamorphose within two months. Voice: an explosive harsh croak.

Lives in burrows in areas with sandy soil, in open woodland and brush. Much of eastern USA from New England to Florida and west to Kentucky and Mississippi, absent from Appalachians and much of Louisiana. Separate population in Texas and Oklahoma.

Plains Spadefoot: bony lump between the eyes. Couch's Spadefoot: yellow-green toad with sickle-shaped spade; shortgrass prairie and brush in Texas, New Mexico and Arizona.

49

PLAINS SPADEFOOT
1½—2½in

A stout toad, with a bony hump between the eyes. Gray-green or brown with lighter stripes on the back. Underside white. On the inner side of each hind foot is a prominent rounded black tubercle, the spade, which is used for digging.

Nocturnal. Makes burrow by digging backwards into soft ground. Eggs laid in temporary pools, after rain, between May and August. Eggs hatch in two days and tadpoles metamorphose into toads in two months. Voice: a grating croak.

Hides by day in burrow in shortgrass prairies where the soil is loose, from southern Alberta and Saskatchewan, south through Great Plains to Texas and New Mexico.

Western Spadefoot and Couch's Spadefoot have no bony hump between the eyes.

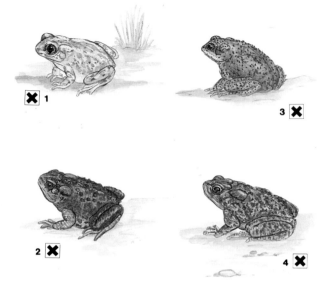

Western Spadefoot (1)

Stout green-brown or gray-green toad, often with a creamy yellow line on each side of back & a black wedge-shaped spade on each hind foot. Voice like purr of cat. Shortgrass prairie, alkaline flats & river valleys in southwestern USA.

Canadian Toad (2)

A small toad, green-brown with red warts and a bony hump on the head between the eyes. Voice a low-pitched trill. Lives on lake & pond margins from Alberta to Manitoba & into central northern USA.

Red-spotted Toad (3)

A small olive-brown toad, with red warts & round parotoid glands. Voice a musical trill. Lives in prairies & deserts, in rocky areas, usually near water. From Texas west to Calif.

Southern Toad (4)

A small toad, gray, brown or reddish in color with conspicuous cranial crests forming knobs in middle of head. Areas with loose sandy soil, in the coastal plain of southeastern USA from N. Carolina to Mississippi.

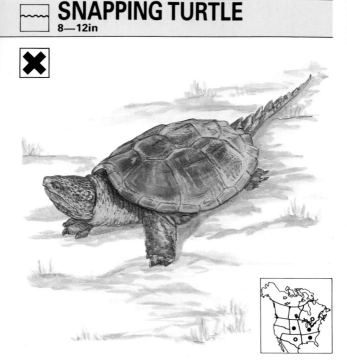

Carapace small, olive or brown and often covered with algae. This turtle has a large head, covered with skin, not scales, and powerful jaws with which it can inflict a serious bite. It has a long tail with saw-like teeth on the upper side.

Hunts at night for crayfish, fishes, salamanders, frogs etc., also feeds on plants. Eggs laid in hole in summer, some distance from the water. Large numbers are caught each year for human consumption.

Lives buried in mud with only eyes exposed, at the bottom of any freshwater body of water, usually where there is abundant vegetation. Eastern and central USA and southern Canada from the Atlantic coast west to the Rocky Mountains.

Alligator Snapping Turtle: largest freshwater turtle, with massive head and strongly hooked beak; has three pronounced rows of keels on carapace.

ALLIGATOR SNAPPING TURTLE

13—26in

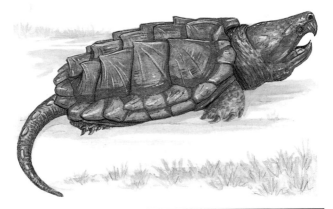

Largest freshwater turtle in the world. It has a small brown or gray carapace with three rows of prominent keels and a long tail. Its head is massive, covered with plates, and with a pronounced hook on the beak. It can give a serious bite.

"Fishes" for prey by lying in wait on bottom, opening its mouth and moving a pink worm-like lure on its tongue. Female lays eggs in hole close to water in summer, the only time she leaves the water, males never do. Caught for human food.

Lives in deep water in rivers, lakes, swamps and sloughs in southeastern USA from Georgia through northern Florida to Texas and up the Mississippi river valley to Indiana, and into Kansas.

Snapping Turtle is smaller, with no hook on its beak and with a much more flattened carapace.

SPINY SOFTSHELL
Male 5—9in; female 6½—18in

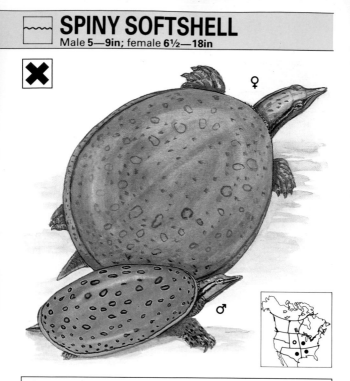

Carapace flat, olive-gray or brown with dark rings on young individuals fading with age, soft and leathery and without scutes. There are spines on the front of the carapace. Females much larger than males. Bites and scratches with sharp claws.

Lies in wait, partly buried in mud for prey, like crayfish, mollusks, frogs and worms, or basks on sandbanks or floating debris. Female lays eggs in deep hole on land near water in summer. Can move fast over land and swim fast in water.

Lives in shallow water in ponds, lakes or rivers. Much of eastern and central USA as far west as Wyoming and Texas, with isolated populations further west; mostly absent from northeast.

Smooth Softshell: no spines on carapace. Florida Softshell: dark brown blotched carapace with blunt tubercles on front; largest and heaviest softshell, found in Florida and Georgia.

Carapace smooth, elongated and highly domed, olive-brown to gray in color and often covered in algae. Head has two light stripes on each side, above and below the eye and barbels on chin and throat. Plastron has single indistinct hinge.

Feeds on bottom on mollusks, crayfish, aquatic insects and carrion, usually at night. Eggs laid in shallow hole dug in loose earth on land, often under rotten stump, in summer. When disturbed this turtle secretes a foul yellowish fluid.

Lives in still or slow-moving shallow water, usually where the bottom is muddy, throughout much of eastern N. America, from Maine to Florida, west to southern Ontario, southern Wisconsin and Texas.

Mud and **Yellow Mud Turtles** lack stripes on sides of head; have two distinct hinges on plastron. Loggerhead Musk Turtle: scutes on carapace overlap, plastron has single hinge.

55

PAINTED TURTLE
4—7in
Eastern Painted

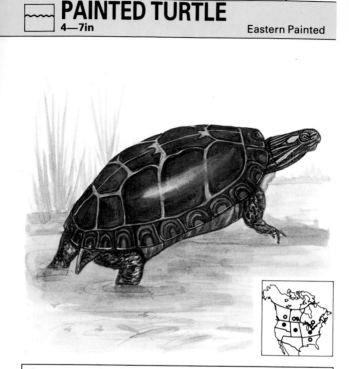

Carapace smooth and oval, often with red or yellow markings on the seams of the scutes and always with red marks on marginal scutes. There are red and yellow stripes on the neck, legs and tail.

May be seen basking in groups on logs or floating amongst lilies. Feeds on wide variety of prey, including mollusks, insects, crustaceans and plants. Eggs laid in shallow cavity on land near water in June or July.

Lives in still or slow-moving shallow waters of lakes, ponds, streams and marshes. Southern B.C. and Washington state, east to Atlantic, southeast to Kansas and Louisiana. Absent from southern coastal plain, central southern and southwestern USA.

Four subspecies. Western Painted Turtle is most colorful, Eastern and Midland Painted Turtles have scutes outlined in yellow and Southern Painted Turtle has red stripe down back.

56

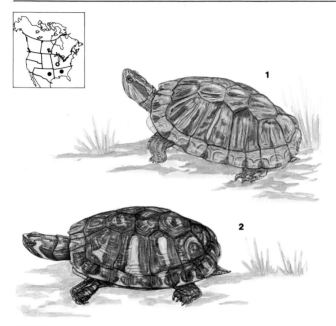

Carapace dark with various patterns, from complex yellowish reticulation to stripes and spots. Plastron yellow with similar markings. There is a prominent red or yellow patch on the head behind each eye.

May be seen basking on logs in groups, one on top of another, or floating with the head just showing in the water. Feeds on a wide variety of prey. Eggs laid in hole on land near water, between April and July. Young sold as pets.

Lives in slow-moving rivers, ponds and lakes where there is abundant vegetation and a muddy bottom. Southeastern USA from Virginia to Texas and west to Illinois and New Mexico.

Three subspecies. Yellow-bellied Slider has yellow stripes on carapace. Red-eared and Cumberland Sliders have reticulated carapace, former has red and latter yellow patch behind eye.

MAP TURTLE
Male **4—6in**; female **7—10in**

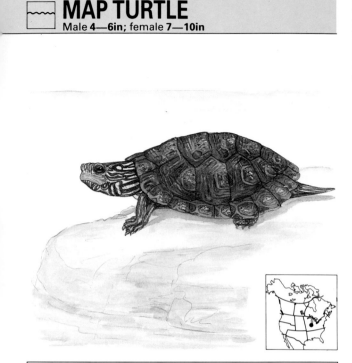

Carapace flattened with a low keel, dark green or brown with a net-like pattern of yellow lines resembling rivers on a map. Narrow yellow stripes on dark skin of head and a yellow spot behind the eye. Females larger than males.

Bask on rocks and floating logs, one on top of another. Feed on mollusks, crayfish and insect larvae. Eggs laid in hole on land by female, between May and July. Timid and shy, quick to enter water if disturbed.

Lives in slow-moving rivers and lakes with abundant vegetation and floating logs. Great Lakes region, east along St Lawrence, south and west along Arkansas and Missouri river systems, south to Tennessee and Arkansas, west to Minnesota.

Several other species of Map Turtles in southeast USA. False Map Turtle lives in Mississippi, Missouri and Ohio river systems, Mississippi Map Turtle in the Mississippi.

MUD TURTLE

3—4in

Carapace smooth and oval in outline, olive to dark brown in color, with 23 marginal scutes, none of which is higher than the others. There are two distinct hinges on the plastron which is yellow or brown in color. May bite.

Feeds on aquatic insects, crustaceans and carrion and may search for food on land. Female lays a few eggs in cavities she has dug in sandy soil or in plant debris in June or July. May exude musky unpleasant odor if disturbed.

Lives in shallow freshwater or brackish slow-moving streams or rivers with abundant vegetation, ponds, marshes and ditches. Often also found on dry land. Connecticut south to Florida and Texas, north to southern Illinois but not in Appalachians.

Other turtles, except **Yellow Mud Turtle,** have 25 marginal scutes. Yellow Mud Turtle: jaw and throat yellow, the ninth and tenth marginal scutes are higher than the others.

59

BLANDING'S TURTLE
5—9in

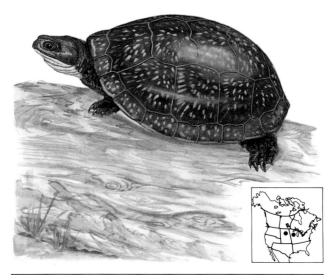

Carapace helmet-shaped, dark brown with many yellow spots. The plastron is hinged so that it can be drawn up close to the carapace, but a notch at rear end prevents complete closure. Underside of jaw and neck bright yellow.

Basks on logs but very timid and re-enters water if disturbed. Retreats into shell if disturbed on land and hisses. Feeds on snails, frogs, worms and fruits. Eggs laid in a hole dug by the female, usually in sandy soil, in June or July.

Lives in ponds, marshes, backwaters of rivers or wanders nearby. Great Lakes region, west to Nebraska.

Spotted Turtle has few spots and plastron is unhinged. **Box Turtles** close up tightly.

60

WOOD TURTLE

5—9in

Carapace brown, each scute looking like a pyramid with concentric growth rings. Plastron yellow with a blotch on the rear margin of each scute, and without a hinge. Underside of throat and legs orange.

Feeds on worms, insects, tadpoles and berries. Eggs laid in a hole dug on land by female in May or June. Often kept as a pet but now much rarer than formerly and protected in some states.

Lives in marshes and swamps, also in woodland streams and may be found some distance from water, in fields, meadows and woods. Northeastern USA and Canada from Nova Scotia to the Great Lakes region and Minnesota, and south to Virginia.

Box Turtles have strongly hinged plastrons and can close their shells tightly.

61

EASTERN BOX TURTLE
4—6in

Carapace keeled and box-like with a high dome, olive-brown in color with a variety of patterns. Plastron hinged so that it can be closed tightly against carapace.

Terrestrial. Hides under rotting logs or in damp vegetation in dry weather, emerging after rain; or soaks in mud. Eggs laid in hole on land between May and July. Young are carnivorous, adults eat slugs, worms, berries and fungi. Kept as pets.

Lives in moist woodland, meadows and prairies in much of eastern and central USA as far north as Missouri and southern Michigan, and west to Texas and Kansas.

Western Box Turtle: similar to Eastern Box Turtle but carapace has no keel. **Wood Turtle:** plastron without hinge, scutes look like pyramids with concentric growth rings.

GOPHER TORTOISE

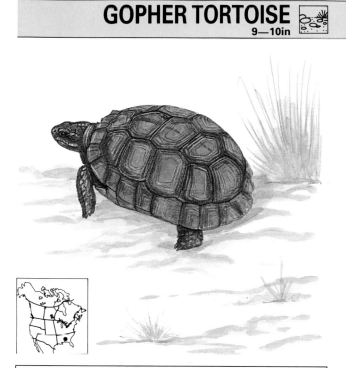

Carapace domed with flattened edges, brown to black, and scutes have concentric growth rings. Hind limbs elephant-like, fore limbs flattened for digging and heavily scaled. They fold against opening of shell to give protection to head and neck.

Terrestrial. Digs a burrow up to 40ft long, with a chamber at the end, which it shares with small mammals, snakes and toads. Grazes on grasses, also eats fruits and berries. Eggs laid in hole, often far from burrow, between April and July.

Found in areas with sandy soil, far from water, in Florida and southern parts of Georgia, Alabama and Mississippi.

Desert Tortoise very similar, lives in arid areas of southern Calif., Nevada and Arizona. Texas Tortoise lives in woodland of southern Texas.

GREEN TURTLE

28—48in

Carapace broad and without a keel, brown in color and often blotched. Limbs paddle-like. There are four large scutes on each side of the back, and one pair of scales between the eyes.

Ocean-going. Found out at sea on long migrations or feeding on turtle grass in shallow waters of continental shelf at river mouths. Females lay large clutches of eggs at night, on sandy Florida beaches.

Continental shelf of southern Atlantic and Pacific Oceans or in open ocean during migrations. Now much rarer than formerly since it has been hunted for its meat and for use in turtle soup.

Hawksbill has two pairs of scales between eyes and carapace scutes overlap; it is an endangered species hunted for its tortoiseshell and meat.

LOGGERHEAD

30—45in

Carapace heart-shaped and keeled, reddish-brown in color and with five scutes on each side of the back. Limbs paddle-like. There are two pairs of scales between the eyes.

Ocean-going. Basks floating on the water. Feeds on clams, crabs, fishes, jellyfishes, sponges and turtle grass. Females lay large clutches of eggs at night on sandy beaches from Texas north, usually to Virginia.

Found in coastal bays, estuaries and out at sea in the warm waters of the southern Atlantic and Pacific Oceans.

Atlantic Ridley is a gravely endangered species, gray in color and growing up to 30in at most. **Green Turtle** and Hawksbill have four scutes on each side of the back.

65

LEATHERBACK
50—70in

Largest turtle. The only sea turtle with a black skin-covered carapace with the texture of hard rubber. It has no scutes but does have seven prominent keels. Limbs paddle-like, without claws.

Ocean-going. Feeds mostly on jellyfish. Female lays eggs on sandy beaches at night, occasionally in Florida, between April and November. An endangered species which was hunted for its oil.

Found in estuaries and out at sea in Atlantic and Pacific Oceans, mostly in warmer southern waters, but also north to B.C. and Newfoundland in summer.

No similar species.

River Cooter (1)
Carapace variously marked with yellow patterns, often in the form of circles & whorls. Lakes & rivers from Virginia south & west to Texas, absent from most of Florida.

Spotted Turtle (2)
Small turtle. Black carapace, head, neck and legs all have yellow spots. Marshes, wet meadows & woods from Maine through coastal plain to northern Florida & west to Michigan & Indiana.

Chicken Turtle (3)
Long striped neck is almost as long as carapace. Shallow ponds & lakes, swamps and ditches. Coastal plain of southeast USA from Virginia to Texas.

False Map Turtle (4)
This turtle has yellow and green lines on the throat that extend forward beyond eye, & a crescent-shaped or bar-shaped yellow mark behind the eye. Lakes, ponds & rivers with abundant vegetation. Mississippi river system & tributaries.

OTHER TURTLES

Western Pond Turtle (1)
Carapace smooth & low, dark brown marked with network of lines & spots radiating from centers of scutes. Marshes, ponds & lakes, also in brackish waters, from southern B.C. to Calif.

Diamondback Terrapin (2)
Carapace low & keeled with deeply grooved growth rings on scutes. Coastal waters, in estuaries & lagoons from Cape Cod south to Texas. Overhunting for meat has caused serious decline in numbers. Now protected.

Yellow Mud Turtle (3)
Underside of head & neck bright yellow. Ninth & tenth marginal scutes higher than eighth. Marshes, ponds & canals with muddy bottoms. Texas north to Kansas.

Smooth Softshell (4)
Flattened, leathery carapace with no scutes. No tubercles or spines on front edge. Rivers, lakes & streams with sandy bottoms. Mississippi river system & its tributaries, also in Alabama river.

Largest reptile in North America. Brown or black with eight rows of enlarged shields running along its back. It has a broad flattened snout. Dangerous.

Emerges from hibernation in April. Makes loud bellowing sound. Feeds on frogs, snakes and small mammals; adults may take deer or cattle. Female lays eggs in round nest, about five feet high, remains nearby till young hatch and then digs them out.

Lives in and beside freshwater ponds, marshes and lakes as well as brackish waters of rivers; digs deep holes or dens which provide water for wildlife in times of drought. Coastal plain of southeastern USA from N. Carolina to Texas.

American Crocodile has long slender snout; lives in mangrove swamps at tip of Florida peninsula.

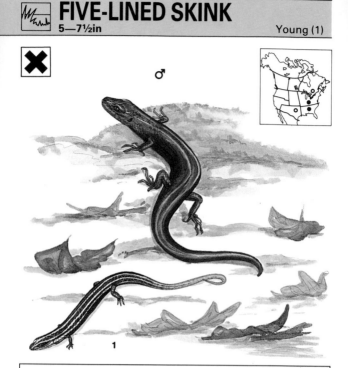

♂

1

Young have five light lines running along length of body; these lines are retained to some extent by adult females but adult males are often uniform brown and may have a red head. There is a row of enlarged scales at the base of the tail.

Active by day. Remains in moist places, under stones or logs, in rotting stumps or piles of leaves on cool days but may be seen sunning itself in the open in warm sunshine. Rarely climbs trees. Feeds on small insects, spiders and worms.

Found in damp woodland, where there is abundant rotting wood or stumps, dead leaves or piles of brush. Eastern USA from southern New England, west to the Great Lakes region and south to Georgia and Texas.

Southeastern Five-lined Skink is similar but does not have enlarged scales at base of tail. Broad-headed Skink is larger and male has a red head. Both species climb trees.

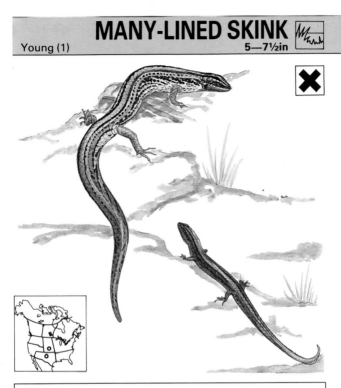

A slender lizard with a wide light stripe on the middle of the back and alternating dark and light stripes running along the length of the sides from head to the base of the tail. Tail blue in juveniles, brown in adults.

Active by day. Hides under debris, broken boards, in prairie dog towns or beneath plants. Feeds on insects.

Found in plains and shortgrass prairies, coniferous woods, vacant urban lots and deserts, usually near moisture, from Arizona and New Mexico north through Colorado into Nebraska and southern South Dakota.

Mountain Skink, from Arizona and Mexico, has a Y-shaped mark on its head. No other skink has a similar pattern of many lines.

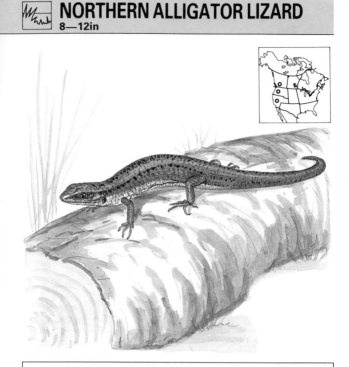

This lizard has a long body and short limbs. There is a fold of skin along the side of the body. Olive-green or bluish in color with a cream-colored underside, striped with dark lines running along the edges of the scales.

Active by day. Hides under logs, loose bark or rocks or in tall grass in more open areas. May be seen sunning itself on logs. Feeds on various insects, spiders, snails and other small animals.

Found along the Pacific coast in coniferous forests, from southern B.C. and Vancouver Island south to Calif. Also in the Rocky Mountains into Montana and south to the Cascades and Sierra Nevada.

Southern Alligator Lizard is similar but lacks dark lines on underside.

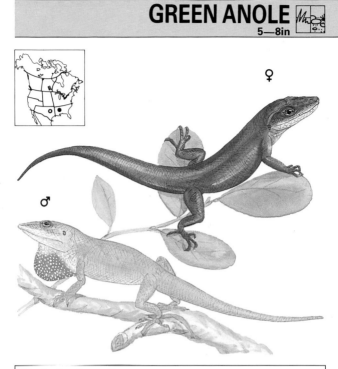

Slender lizard, usually green in color but can change color to brown like a chameleon. Male has pink throatfan—an extensible flap of skin used in territorial and courtship displays.

Very active by day, males frequently display to each other or fight amongst themselves. May be seen stalking their prey, like flies and moths. Usually green when resting in shade or fighting, but turn brown in the sun.

Seen on fences, shrubs, vines and trees, sometimes on the walls of old buildings or on the ground, often in shady places. Southern Virginia south and west to the Florida keys and Texas.

Several other anoles live in peninsular Florida. Brown Anole has a yellow or orange throatfan with a white line in the center.

Widely distributed and varying greatly in color and pattern within this large range. It may be gray or brown and may or may not have stripes along its back. Blue markings form a wedge on each side of the throat of the male.

Active by day. Eastern forms more often seen on trees and fences while prairie and western forms live on the ground or in brush. Feeds on a variety of insects and spiders as well as other small animals.

Found in a wide variety of habitats from prairies to mountains, in woods, rocky and sandy areas, on log piles, in brush heaps and on buildings or fences. From Delaware south to Florida and west to Arizona.

Several subspecies, varying in range and habitat, including Northern and Southern Fence, Prairie and Plateau Lizards. **Western Fence Lizard** male has single blue throat patch.

A slender lizard with a long tail. It has a broad brown stripe on its back and three white to yellow stripes running along the length of each side. There are eight rows of large scales on the belly. Throat of male green or blue, of female white.

Active by day, most often seen in mornings. This is an agile lizard which can run fast to avoid danger. It digs its own burrow. Feeds on soft-bodied insects and spiders.

Found in a variety of habitats, dry flat or foothill areas with loose sandy soil, open woods and grasslands. Delaware west to Colorado and New Mexico, and throughout southeastern USA. Also north to Wisconsin in the Mississippi river system.

Desert Grassland Whiptail has olive green tail, lives in New Mexico and Arizona. Texas Spotted Whiptail: dark areas between light stripes on side contain spots, found in Texas.

75

A ground-living lizard, gray-green to brown with yellowish sides and light stripes on back and sides. It has a black bar on the shoulder and a rust-colored patch in the armpit. Scales on the backs of the thighs are gray, smooth and granular.

Active by day. Feeds on a wide variety of insects. Remains close to rock piles, brush heaps or rodent burrows in which it can hide if danger threatens.

Found in open ground with scattered plants in sagebrush, pinyon-juniper areas and open coniferous woodland. Western USA from Calif. east to northern Arizona and New Mexico, north to Washington state and Montana.

Western Fence Lizard is larger, has no rust-color in armpits, has dark spots along length of the back and has no shoulder bar; male has single blue throat patch.

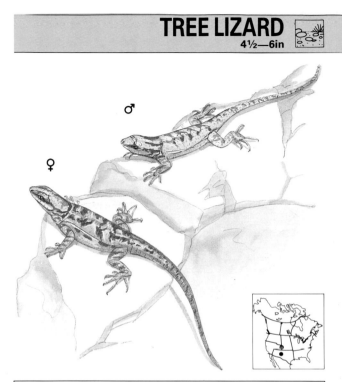

♂

♀

Brown or gray lizard with blotched back. Male has yellowish or blue throat and sides. Strip of small scales in middle of back separates two strips of large scales; large scales also found in skin folds along sides. It has fold of skin across throat.

Active by day. Usually seen in a vertical position on a tree, rock or even a building; it is good at dodging and keeping the tree or rock between it and any pursuer. Most likely to be seen in morning or evening searching for insects.

Found in variety of habitats from sea level to mountains, in woodland, canyons and deserts. From southeastern Calif. and Arizona east to Texas, north to Utah and western Colorado, and into Wyoming.

Side-blotched Lizard: scales on back uniformly small in size. Long-tailed Brush Lizard has a single strip of large scales along the length of the back.

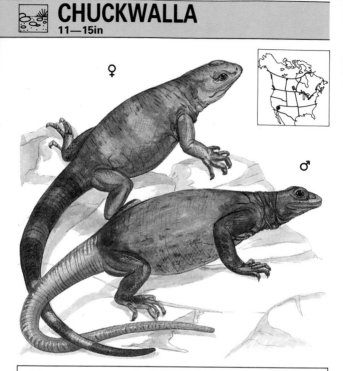

A large fat-bodied lizard with loose folds of skin on neck and sides. It has a long tail, thick at the base. Color varies: head and shoulders of male black, body reddish; females and young often crossbanded, with olive-gray bodies.

Active by day. This lizard is herbivorous, browsing on the tender buds, flowers and leaves of plants. Wary and secretive, it disappears into a crevice if disturbed and can inflate itself so that it is almost impossible to get out.

Found in rocky areas, on barren hillsides and mountains, and on lava beds, where there are many crevices for hiding places. Southeastern Calif., western Arizona, southern tips of Nevada and Utah.

No other similar lizards grow as large as this one.

GILA MONSTER
16—22in

A large heavy lizard with bead-like scales. Its body is irregularly marked with patterns and blotches of black and buff yellow, orange or yellow-pink. Underside of head and feet are darker. It has a venomous, though rarely fatal, bite.

Mostly active at dusk and nocturnal. Moves slowly and awkwardly but digs well. Feeds on birds, small mammals and eggs. When biting, this lizard chews the wound like a bulldog, injecting the poison into it.

Found in arid and semi-arid areas, where there is sparse vegetation like cacti, mesquite or creosote bushes, and some water. From the southern tip of Nevada south into Arizona.

No similar species.

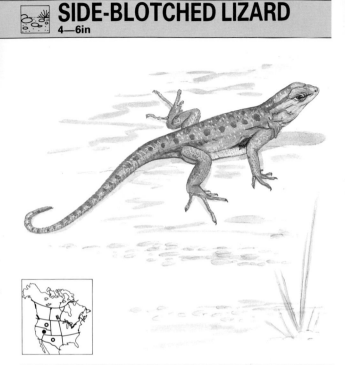

A ground-living lizard with a fold of skin across the throat. The scales of this fold and those of the back are all small and uniform. Brown in color with blotches on the back and a single blue or black spot on the side behind the fore leg.

Active by day. Seen throughout the year; hides under plants in hottest months. Feeds mostly on large insects like grasshoppers, beetles and moths.

Found from sea level to mountains in arid areas, deserts, washes, canyons and slopes, usually where soil is gravelly and there is sparse vegetation. Calif. and Arizona north to Utah, northwest to Washington state. Also in New Mexico and Texas.

Western Fence Lizard and **Tree Lizard** lack dark spots on the side. Tree Lizard has strips of larger scales on the back.

TEXAS HORNED LIZARD

2½—4½in

A flat-bodied, gray or brown lizard with spines at the back of the head, the central two spines longest. It has a short tail and two rows of pointed fringe scales along each side of the body.

Active by day. Usually seen on very hot days, running fast or sheltering in rock piles or beneath cactus or mesquite. Feeds on insects, especially on large ants, and spiders. Kept as pets but often die from lack of warmth and/or correct food.

Found in flat open areas, up to about 6000ft above sea level, where the vegetation is sparse. From southern Texas north to Kansas and in New Mexico.

Several other horned lizards. **Short-horned Lizard** has a deep notch at back of head and short spines all the same length. Desert Horned Lizard has short spines all the same length.

COLLARED LIZARD
8—12in

A brightly colored, stout-bodied lizard with a large head and a long tail. It has a conspicuous double, black and white collar around its neck, along with other variable stripes and spots on the body. The inside of the mouth is dark.

Active by day. When threatened it runs on all four legs until it attains some speed, then runs more or less upright on back legs only. Aggressive when cornered and will bite hard. Feeds on large insects and small lizards.

Found in arid and semi-arid areas on rock piles, in canyons and gullies from eastern Calif., east to Arkansas and Missouri, and north to southern Idaho and Oregon.

Reticulate Collared Lizard has rows of black spots across body, found in southern Texas.

LEOPARD LIZARD

8—15in

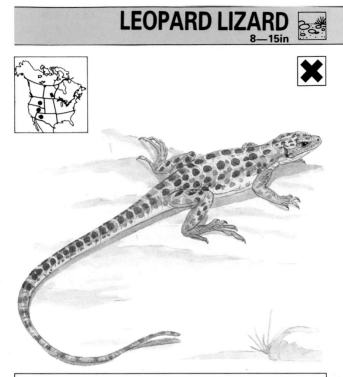

A long slender lizard with a large head and a long tail. It is gray or brown in color, with many dark spots and a lighter underside.

Active by day. Lies in shade of plant in ambush for prey. Runs fast with fore limbs raised, darting from one plant to another or chasing prey. Feeds on large insects like grasshoppers, also on other lizards and berries. Aggressive if cornered.

Found in flat arid and semi-arid areas with sparse vegetation, where the soil is sandy, or of coarse gravel or hardpan. From southern Oregon and Idaho, south to Calif. and southeast to Arizona and the western tip of Texas.

Collared Lizard is brightly colored, with two black collars.

83

LESSER EARLESS LIZARD
4—5in

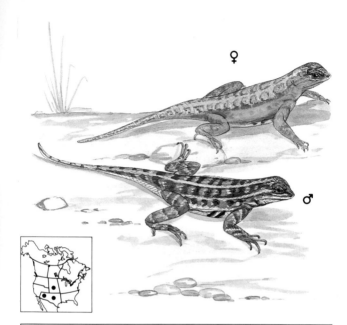

A small plump lizard with granular scales on the back. Gray or brown in color, often with four rows of dark spots running along body, but color changes with background. Male has black bars on side of belly. It has no external ear openings.

Active by day. This lizard will bury itself in sandy soil during the heat of the day or stay in the shade of plants. Feeds on insects and spiders. Does not run very fast.

Found in arid and prairie regions where the soil is sandy or gravelly and there is sparse vegetation, in dry streambeds or fields and in Kansas chalk beds. From New Mexico east to Texas and north to Nebraska.

Greater Earless Lizard has black bars under the tail. **Side-blotched Lizard** has external ear openings, a fold across the throat and a dark spot on each side behind the fore leg.

84

BANDED GECKO

4½—6in

Skin soft, covered with fine granular scales. Body rounded, creamy in color and banded in brown.

Nocturnal and may be seen on highways at night. Hides by day under stones, in crevices beneath rocks, often under boards, cans and other garbage near highway. Feeds on insects and spiders.

Found in deserts and arid areas, in canyons and foothills of southern Calif., Nevada and New Mexico.

Texas Banded Gecko is very similar to Banded Gecko and lives in similar habitats, but is found in southern Texas and southern New Mexico.

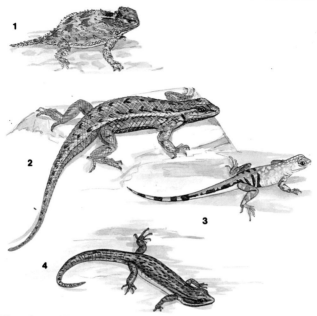

Short-horned Lizard (1)
Flat-bodied lizard with deep notch at back of head, flanked by blunt spines. One row of pointed fringe scales along each side. Sandy & rocky areas, short-grass prairies, in much of western USA but absent from Calif., Nevada, Oklahoma & Texas.

Western Fence Lizard (2)
Brown or gray lizard with blotches on back. Male has blue underside & single blue throat patch. Fence posts, rocks & in canyons, usually in wooded areas, throughout much of Rockies of USA.

Greater Earless Lizard (3)
This lizard has black bands across the underside, with similar bands beneath the tail. It has smooth granular scales & no external ear openings. Lives in rocky areas in southern Texas, New Mexico & Arizona.

Desert Night Lizard (4)
Color varies with background. It has no eyelids. In arid areas, usually in association with plants like Spanish Bayonets & Joshua Trees, often amongst fallen leaves & branches. Southern Calif., Nevada, Utah & Arizona.

Ground Skink (1)
Small brown lizard with a dark stripe on the back. There is a transparent "window" in the movable lower eyelid. Woodland floor in leaf litter, from New Jersey south to Florida & west to Texas & Kansas.

Western Skink (2)
Slender elongate lizard with brown back & two light stripes on each side running along the length of the body. Open woods & grassland with cover in the form of logs & rocks. Western USA from southern B.C. to coastal Calif., east to Idaho & Utah.

Western Whiptail (3)
Slender lizard with four to eight longitudinal stripes & many brown transverse bars & spots. Arid & semi-arid areas with sparse vegetation or sagebrush from Calif. to Idaho & east to Utah, also southeast to Arizona & southern Texas.

Southern Alligator Lizard (4)
Brown in color with dark crossbands & grayish undersides. There is a fold of skin along each side. Oak woodland & chaparral, grassland, usually in cover of brush heaps or logs. Southern Washington state to Calif.

SLENDER GLASS LIZARD
20—40in

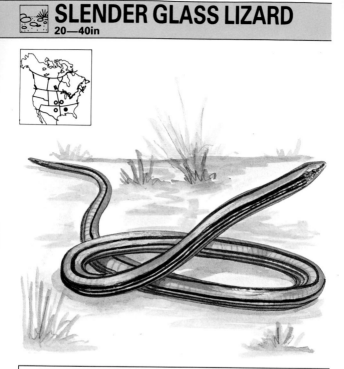

Shiny, legless lizard with movable eyelids and external ear openings. It feels stiff to the touch and has a long fragile tail. There are dark lines on sides of body below the lateral groove and white marks in the middles of scales on the back.

Active by day. Feeds on insects, insect grubs and spiders. Usually found above ground but hibernates in burrows.

Found in dry open woodlands and dry grassland from Virginia west to Kansas and Texas, south to Florida.

Eastern Glass Lizard has white-edged scales on back and no dark stripes on sides, lives in coastal plain of southeast USA. Snakes have no eyelids and no external ear openings.

QUEEN SNAKE

15—24in

The back of this relatively slender snake is brown and the underside is yellow with four dark lines; there is also a yellow band on each side and it has a yellow nose. It has a small head. Scales are keeled and in 19 rows.

Active both by day and at night. Hides beneath rocks or branches or amongst debris beside water. Discharges musk if threatened but seldom bites. Feeds on crayfish, especially those that have just shed their skins.

Found in or beside swift-flowing streams and small rivers, lakes, ponds and ditches from the Great Lakes east to Pennsylvania and south to northern Florida. Absent from southeastern coastal plain.

Garter Snakes usually have a light stripe along the middle of the back.

NORTHERN WATER SNAKE
24—42in

Gray to brown snake with darker crossbands on neck, darker blotches on the middle and rear of the body. No dark line between angle of jaw and eye.

Active any time of day or night. Feeds on amphibians and fishes. Aggressive if cornered and bites bleed freely, due to anticoagulant in the saliva.

Found in and near marshes, streams, ditches, canals, ponds, lakes and saltmarshes throughout much of eastern USA, west to Wisconsin and Colorado, but only to Mississippi in the south. Absent from southeastern coastal plain.

Some Southern Water Snakes resemble Northern Water Snakes but have dark line from mouth to eye. Blotched form of **Plain-bellied Water Snake** occurs from western Missouri to Texas.

BROWN SNAKE

9—13in

A small brown or yellow-brown snake with a lighter band running along the center of the back, bordered by two parallel rows of dark spots. Scales are keeled and in 17 rows.

Usually active by day, but nocturnal in hot weather. Often hide in groups under boards or logs, in leaves or trash piles, usually in moist places. If caught it expels musk but does not bite. Feeds on worms, slugs, snails, insects and frogs.

Found in city vacant lots, parks and gardens; in rural areas in marshes, swamps and moist woodland. Throughout eastern USA west to Minnesota, Kansas and Texas. Also in southern Quebec.

Worm Snake and **Ground Snake** have smooth scales and no rows of spots on their backs. Worm Snake has red-pink underside.

91

COMMON GARTER SNAKE
18—26in   Eastern (1); Red-sided (2)

Back green, brown or black; underside light green or yellow.
Light stripe runs down each side on second and third row of scales
and other stripes on back are often broken by black squares.
Seven scales on upper lip. Scales keeled, in 19 rows.

Active by day. Hunts in wet vegetation for prey, amphibians,
small mammals, birds and worms. May exude an unpleasant
musky scent and attempts to bite if cornered. Hibernates in large
groups in north.

Found in a wide variety of habitats near water, in fields,
meadows, prairies, marshes, ditches and roadsides, city lots and
gardens throughout eastern USA and southern Canada, north and
northwest USA and Calif.

Other garter snakes within the same area have side stripes which
involve the fourth row of scales. Such snakes include the **Eastern
Ribbon Snake** and **Plains Garter Snake**.

Dark snake with white flecks, a light stripe on each side on the second and third scale row, and a well-defined light stripe along middle of back. Eight scales on upper lip, sixth and seventh larger than others. Scales keeled, in 19-21 rows.

Active by day. Feeds on mice, amphibians, lizards, slugs and worms, as well as fishes. If threatened this snake will attempt to escape into the water.

Found in long grass of damp meadows and woodland clearings, chaparral, near ponds, lakes and streams, from sea level to high mountains. From B.C. to Manitoba and south to northern Calif., Arizona and New Mexico.

Northwestern Garter Snake usually has bright red or yellow stripe in middle of back. Western Aquatic Garter Snake has little or no stripe in the middle of its back.

RUBBER BOA
14—30in

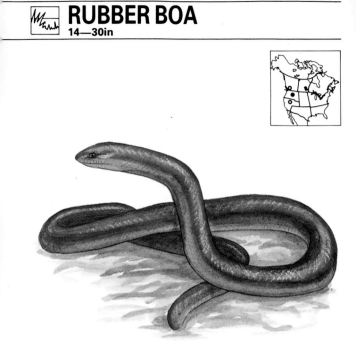

Sometimes called "Two-headed Snake", since head and tail are both blunt. Scales on back of head are large. Males have small but obvious spurs either side of anus. Brown or green in color with yellowish underside and no pattern.

Active at dusk and nocturnal. Hides by day in or under rotting logs, under moist debris, bark or rocks, in damp sand. Kills its prey, usually small mammals and lizards, by constricting them.

Found in or near damp coniferous woodland from southern B.C. south to northern Calif. and east to northwestern Wyoming and Utah.

Rosy Boa has three broad longitudinal reddish stripes, no enlarged scales on head; found in arid areas of Calif. and Arizona.

WORM SNAKE

8—14in

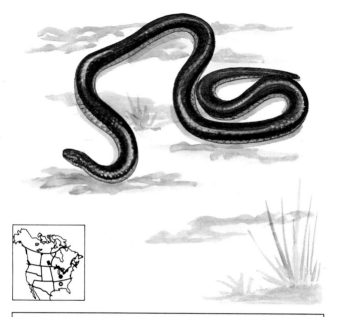

A small glossy snake with a dark brown or black back without any pattern and a red-pink underside. Tail short and pointed. Scales are smooth and in 13 rows.

Hides under rotten logs and stumps, rocks and woodland debris or in damp soil. Feeds on worms and slugs. Remains deep underground in dry or cold weather and most likely to be seen in spring.

Found in damp woods and nearby fields from southern New England, south to northern Georgia and west to southern Iowa, Oklahoma and Louisiana.

Earth Snake is plain brown with light grayish underside. **Ground Snake** is usually patterned and without a red underside. **Brown Snake** has light stripe on back, bordered by dark spots.

95

RINGNECK SNAKE
10—20in   Southern (1); Prairie (2)

Small slender snake with smooth scales. It has a distinctive yellow or orange ring around its neck and a bright yellow or orange underside with a variable pattern of black spots. The back varies in color from olive to brown or black.

Nocturnal. Hides under logs or bark and amongst rocks. Some forms may coil up to show colored underside if unearthed and it secretes a pungent substance to deter predators. Feeds on salamanders, lizards, young snakes and worms.

Found in woodland, rocky hillsides, grassland and chaparral, often near water. Nova Scotia south to Florida, west to Arizona and north along the Pacific coast. Mostly absent from northwest and northern central USA and Canada.

Several subspecies. Prairie Ringneck has random black spots, Mississippi Ringneck two rows of black spots, Southern Ringneck one row of black spots. Northern Ringneck has no spots.

MILK SNAKE

Eastern (1); Red (2)

14—50in

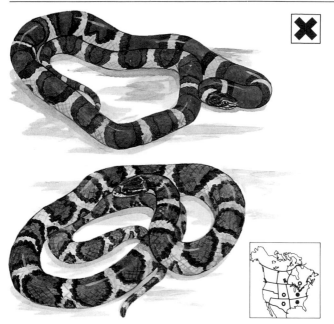

Slender snake. It has a gray or brown body with red, black and yellow rings, or with reddish-brown black-bordered blotches. The colors red and yellow do not touch each other. Scales are smooth and in 19–23 rows.

Usually only comes out at night. Hides by day in burrows, rotting logs, stumps, beneath boards, in barns. Kills its prey by constriction, small mammals, snakes, lizards and amphibians, also eats eggs.

Found in a wide variety of habitats from prairies to woodlands, barrens, rocky hillsides, farmland, bottomlands and bogs, from sea level to mountain slopes. Maine and Quebec south to Florida and west to Rockies through much of the USA.

Several subspecies, including Eastern, Red, Louisiana, Central Plains and Pale Milk Snakes, varying in pattern and range. The venomous **Coral Snake** has red and yellow rings touching.

97

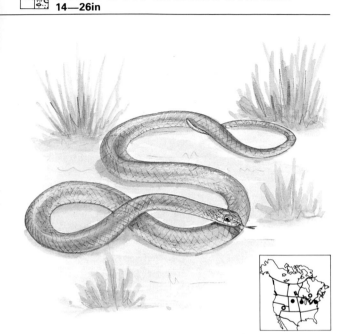

Small smooth snake with long tail; bright green in color with whitish underside. The scales are smooth and arranged in 15 rows.

Active by day. A secretive, gentle snake which seldom bites even if caught. Well camouflaged in grassland. Feeds on spiders and insects.

Found in meadows, pastures and marshes from sea level to mountain areas in northern USA and southeastern Canada, from the Atlantic to Minnesota and south as far as N. Carolina. Also scattered through the midwest.

Rough Green Snake has keeled scales in 17 rows, giving it a rough appearance; it lives in trees in southeastern USA.

RACER

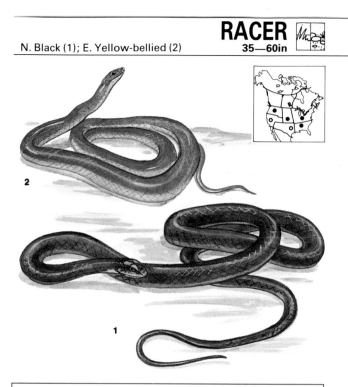

Large, slender, fast-moving snake with smooth lustrous scales, in 15 rows at the anus. Color is very variable, from brown or black to blue on the back, yellow to white or gray on the underside.

Active by day. Hides in brush piles, walls and rocks, trash piles, often near water. Aggressive and can give vicious bite. May be seen streaking across roads or grassland, head held high. Eats frogs and toads, lizards, small mammals and birds.

Found in a wide variety of habitats, from prairie grassland to brush and woodland, from sea level to mountains. Atlantic to Pacific coasts in USA but mostly absent from southeast and northern central states. Also in southern B.C.

Eleven subspecies. Yellow-bellied Racer lives in midwest, Blue Racer in Great Lakes area. Black Racers of eastern USA similar to black **Common** and **Prairie Kingsnakes** and black **Rat Snake**.

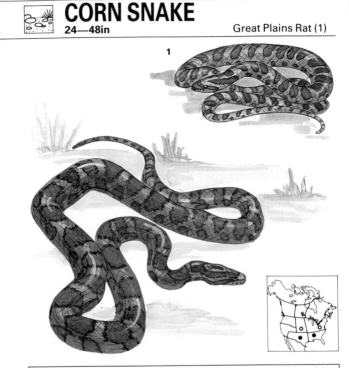

Long slender snake, yellow-brown to brown or gray in color with brown to reddish black-edged saddle-shaped blotches along the length of the back. It has a spear-shaped mark on its head and black bars or checkered marks on the underside.

Active at dusk and nocturnal. Hides by day in rodent burrows or under cover. Feeds on small mammals and birds. May be found in old houses in the south. Gentle and makes a good pet.

Found in woodland and grassland, on rocky hillsides and around buildings. From New Jersey south to Florida and west to Nebraska and New Mexico.

Two forms: Corn Snake is eastern form with red blotches on yellow background. Great Plains Rat Snake has brown or olive blotches on gray background.

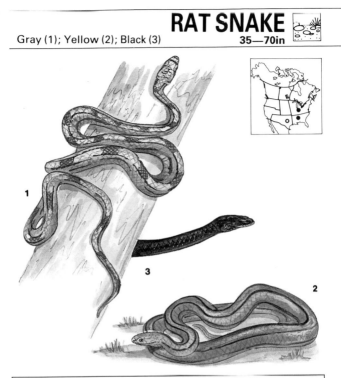

Three forms: back of snake may be plain black, blotched or striped. Blotched form is light gray or brown with dark blotches; striped form is red, yellow or gray with four dark stripes. Scales are weakly keeled and in 25–33 rows.

Active in the day in spring and fall, at night in summer. A good climber, most often seen in trees and shrubs, on stumps or rafters of buildings. Kills by constricting prey which includes frogs, lizards and small mammals.

Found in woods and forests, rocky hillsides, farmyards and barns (Yellow Rat Snake is sometimes called Chicken Snake), from Ontario south to Florida and west to Texas and Iowa.

Texas and Gray Rat Snake (from Mississippi valley): both gray or yellow with brown saddle-shaped blotches. Yellow Rat Snake: striped, from southeast USA. Black Rat Snake: northeast USA.

COMMON KINGSNAKE
30—70in Eastern (1); Calif. (2); Speckled (3)

Large snake with a small head, very variable in color and pattern. It may be plain black or brown, or have a speckled appearance, or be blotched or striped. Scales are smooth and shiny, in 19—25 rows.

Active by day, especially near dusk and dawn, but nocturnal in hotter areas. Found on the ground, in rodent burrows, or may climb trees. Usually gentle. Kills its prey by constriction, other snakes, lizards, small mammals and birds, also eggs.

Found in a wide variety of habitats from woodland to meadows, prairies, chaparral and rocky hillsides. All southern USA from Oregon in the west to New Jersey in the east.

Several subspecies including Eastern (black with white chain pattern), Black (an eastern form), Speckled (from Miss valley), Desert (a blotched form) and Calif. (striped).

102

GOPHER & PINE SNAKE

Gt. Basin Gopher (1); N. Pine (2)   **48—72in**

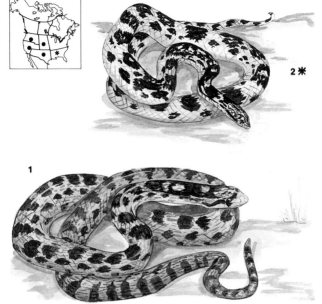

2 ✳

1

Powerful snakes with small heads and keeled scales, usually in 29 rows. Pine Snake is whitish with row of black blotches; Gopher Snake is light brown with row of brown blotches. Both have other smaller blotches along the sides.

Usually active by day but may be nocturnal in hot weather. Hide in rodent burrows, under stones or logs and dig into loose soil. Feed on small mammals and birds, which are killed by constriction, and on eggs.

Pine Snakes live in dry sandy areas with pine woods in eastern USA, from New Jersey south to Florida. Gopher Snakes live in wide variety of habitats, woodland, chaparral and grassland throughout western USA, except the northwest.

These two snakes are members of the same species, together with another subspecies, the Bullsnake. **Bullsnakes** are yellowish in color with red or brown blotches.

STRIPED WHIPSNAKE
30—60in

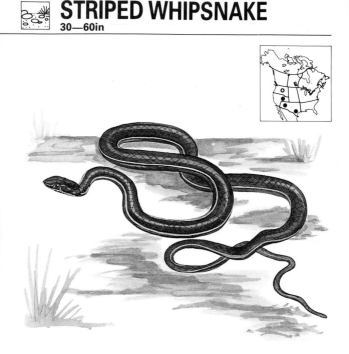

A long slender, grayish or brownish snake, with two or more light stripes along each side. These stripes may be continuous or broken.

Active by day, hunting small mammals, lizards and other snakes. It hunts with its head held high and quickly sees any potential enemy, streaking away to hide in a burrow or crevice if threatened.

Found in rocky, brush-covered foothills, sagebrush flats, pinyon-juniper country, yellow pine-oak forests, grasslands from southern Washington state southeast through Nevada and Utah to Arizona, New Mexico and southern Texas.

Calif. Striped Racer has single yellow stripe on each side; lives on western side of Sierra Nevada in chaparral and open forests.

COACHWHIP

Eastern (1); Red (2); Western (3) **36—60in**

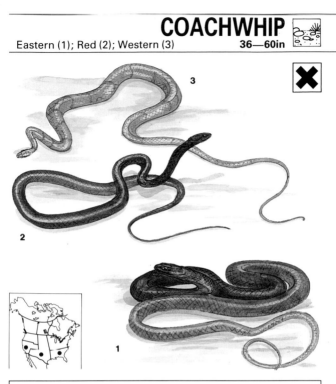

Large, fast-moving, agile snake with long thin tail. Eastern form has dark brown head and neck, the color becoming lighter towards the tail. Western forms reddish or yellowish in color, with little pattern. Scales smooth, in 17 rows, 13 in tail.

Active by day, mostly in morning and late afternoon. Very fast-moving and may climb into tree to avoid pursuit. Aggressive if cornered and strikes repeatedly. Feeds on small mammals, lizards, snakes and large insects.

Found in dry upland areas, dry fields and grasslands, flatwoods, prairies, sagebrush and mesquite areas, and semi-arid regions across southern USA from N. Carolina to Calif.

Eastern form found from N. Carolina to Texas and Kansas; Western is light brown form from midwest; Red form found from Calif. to Arizona. Also several other local western forms.

EASTERN HOGNOSE SNAKE
20—30in

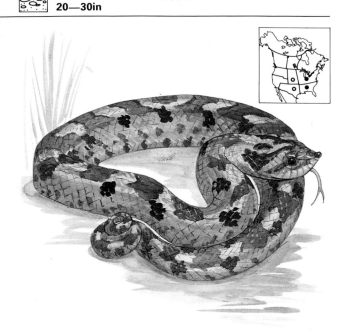

Thick-bodied snake, very variable in color. It may be uniformly brown, black, gray or green or have gray, brown or black blotches. Underside of tail lighter than belly. It has an upturned snout and the scales are keeled.

Active by day. If threatened, it puffs itself up with air, flattens its head and hisses. If the enemy is undeterred it rolls over and "plays dead," and will do so again if righted. Feeds on amphibians, lizards, small mammals and birds.

Found in dry sandy areas, on hillsides, in open woodland and in fields. From New Hampshire south to Florida, west to Minnesota and Texas.

Southern Hognose Snake has sharply upturned snout, belly and tail underside are uniformly gray. **Western Hognose Snake** has sharply upturned snout and black patches on underside.

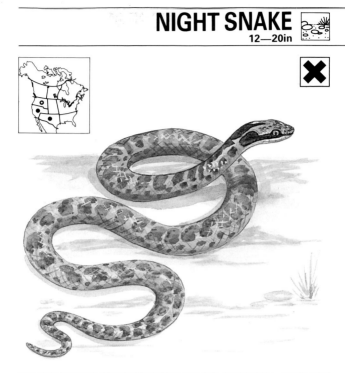

A slender snake, gray or light brownish in color with many gray or brown blotches on the back. There are two large blotches on the sides of the neck which may fuse with a third at the back of the head. Scales smooth.

Mostly nocturnal. Hides under rocks or bark or in sandy soil. Captures small lizards or amphibians which are subdued by the venom in the fangs at the back of the mouth. Not dangerous to people.

Found in arid and semi-arid areas, dry hillsides, deserts, plains and chaparral, from Washington state south through eastern Oregon and Nevada to southern Calif. and east to Texas.

Glossy Snake lacks blotches on neck and has black line running from eye to angle of jaw.

107

HARMLESS EASTERN SNAKES

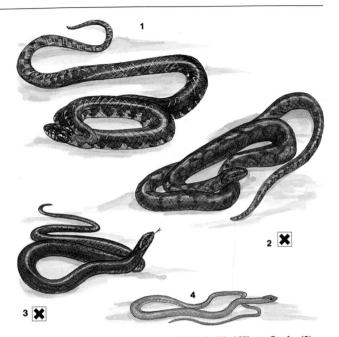

Mud Snake (1)
Blue-black snake with bars on sides & underside. Sharp spine on tail. Scales smooth. Lake and pond margins, slow-moving streams, marshes with abundant vegetation in coastal plain of southeastern USA & Mississippi valley.

Diamondback Water Snake (2)
The only water snake with a dark network-like pattern on its back. Brownish in color. Marshes, ditches, lake margins & rivers. Mississippi river system, west to Texas, Oklahoma & Kansas.

Plain-bellied Water Snake (3)
Plain dark brownish or grayish snake with a red or yellow underside. In vegetation near swamps, ponds, lakes or bayous in southeastern USA. Coastal plain, Mississippi valley & west in river valleys into Texas, Oklahoma & Kansas.

Rough Green Snake (4)
Slender snake with long tail. Bright green with keeled scales which give it a rough appearance. Lives in bushes & small trees near water in eastern USA south of New Jersey & west to Kansas.

HARMLESS EASTERN SNAKES

Scarlet Snake (1)
Wide red saddle-shaped blotches separate much narrower black-edged, yellow blotches. Underside is yellowish. Scales smooth. Burrows in sandy soils of forest areas in southeastern USA.

Smooth Earth Snake (2)
Small, smooth, gray or brown snake with a lighter whitish underside. Damp deciduous woodland & old fields under bark or logs. Southeastern USA, west to Texas & Iowa.

Red-bellied Snake (3)
Small snake, plain brown or gray with red underside and often with narrow darker stripes along back. Mountain woods and bogs, hiding under stones, leaves & logs throughout eastern USA and southeast Canada.

Eastern Ribbon Snake (4)
Slender dark snake with three bright yellow stripes. Side stripe is on scale rows three & four. Shallow water of marshes, ponds & lake margins throughout most of eastern USA & southern Ontario.

HARMLESS WESTERN SNAKES

Plains Garter Snake (1)
Bright yellow or orange stripe on back; side stripes on third & fourth scale rows & square black spots below side stripes. Prairie river valleys, near ponds & sloughs, wet meadows. Indiana south to Ohio & west to Rockies, into southern Canada.

Fox Snake (2)
Light brown snake with large brown or black blotches on back & sides. Scales keeled. Prairies, marshes & fields from western Great Lakes region to S. Dakota & Nebraska.

Prairie Kingsnake (3)
Variable, brownish with dark-edged brownish or greenish blotches on the back & smaller blotches on the sides. Prairies, farmland, open woods & hillsides in southeastern & southern central USA from Texas & Kansas eastwards.

Bullsnake (4)
Large yellowish snake with large red or brown blotches in a row in the middle of the back, and smaller ones on the sides. Scales keeled. Dry prairies and plains from Great Lakes region west to Alberta & south to Texas.

HARMLESS WESTERN SNAKES

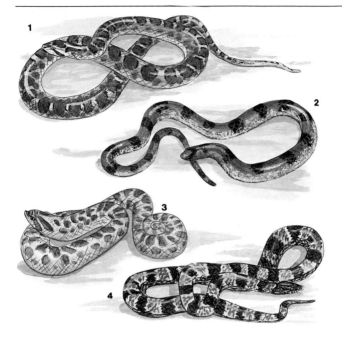

Glossy Snake (1)
Smooth glossy snake with brown or gray blotches on its back which is light brown in color. Sandy arid areas, sagebrush & chaparral. Southwest USA east to Texas.

Ground Snake (2)
Small, smooth snake with broad, flattened head. Varies in color from gray to brown or red with a back stripe, dark bands or blotches. Dry places, prairies, hillsides, under rocks or buried in soil. Southern USA from Calif. to Texas & Oklahoma.

Western Hognose Snake (3)
Heavy snake with an upturned snout on its head. Brown with darker blotches on back & sides. Dry prairies with sandy soil from southern Alberta & Manitoba to Texas & New Mexico.

Long-nosed Snake (4)
This snake has a long cream-colored snout. It has large dark white-edged blotches on a pinkish background. Dry prairies, chaparral and brush, from Calif. to Texas.

COTTONMOUTH
24—48in
or WATER MOCCASIN

Large dark water snake; usually brown or black with darker crossbands which have irregular edges. Head is flattened and there is a dark stripe from eye to corner of mouth. Inside of mouth is white. Facial pit is present between eye and nostril.

Active both by day and at night. Aggressive and will remain coiled and poised ready to strike if disturbed. Highly toxic venom and large fangs combine to make this a dangerous snake. Lies in ambush for small mammals, lizards, birds, amphibians.

Found in swamps and bayous, ditches, irrigation canals and ponds, often coiled up beside water waiting for prey. Coastal plain of southeastern USA from Virginia to Texas and north along the Mississippi river valley to Indiana.

Harmless water snakes have no facial pits but are difficult to distinguish from Cottonmouth in the field. Avoidance of any snake which could be a Cottonmouth is advisable.

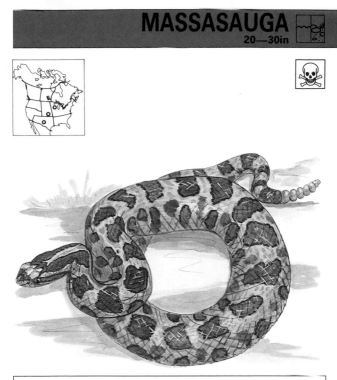

One of the smaller rattlesnakes, brown with a row of large dark, white-edged blotches on its back, and rows of smaller blotches on its sides. It has a medium-sized rattle. There are nine large plate-like scales on the top of the head.

Nocturnal or active on dull days. Basks near water or hides in dense vegetation, amongst mesquite or juniper in the west. Relatively unaggressive and only rattles if annoyed but bite and venom dangerous. Feeds on frogs, small mammals and birds.

Found in marshes, swamps, on the edges of streams and ponds in the east; wet prairies, sagebrush and arid grasslands in the west. From the Great Lakes region southwest to Texas and Arizona. Now relatively rare in much of this range.

Pigmy Rattlesnake has long slender tail and tiny rattle, sounds like insect buzzing. All other rattlesnakes have small scales on the tops of their heads.

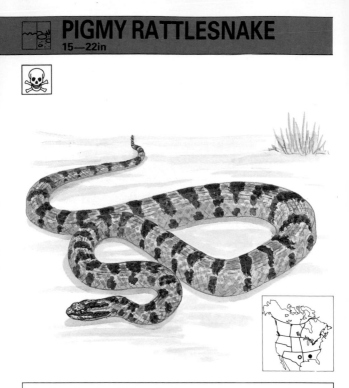

Small rattlesnake with long slender tail and very small rattle which sounds like an insect buzzing. Gray or reddish in color, with a row of large blotches on its back and other blotches on its sides. It has nine large plate-like scales on top of head.

Basks in warm sunshine. Unpredictable, may be aggressive if disturbed, striking without warning; or it may be lethargic. Its bite is dangerous if left untreated. Feeds on small mammals, lizards and birds.

Found in a variety of habitats from dry sandy prairie grassland or pine woodland to wet marshes and lake margins. Southern USA from N. Carolina south to Florida and west to Oklahoma and Texas.

Massasauga has larger tail and much larger rattle. All other rattlesnakes have small scales on the tops of their heads.

114

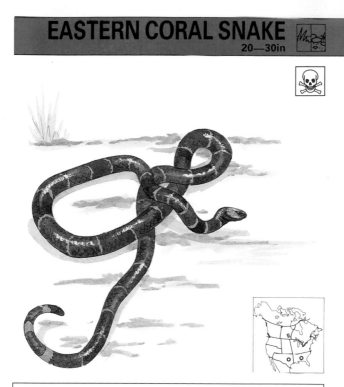

A glossy snake banded with rings of red, yellow and black; the red ring has a yellow band on each side. Head is blunt and black, with a band of yellow behind the eyes.

Active mostly by day, especially in morning. Burrows into soil or hides under logs or rocks. Feeds on small snakes, lizards and amphibians. Snake should be avoided, venom highly toxic, though fangs are at back of mouth and it is slow to bite.

Found in a variety of habitats, open pine woods in sandy soil, lake margins and hardwood hammocks, but usually near water. Southeastern USA in coastal plain from N. Carolina to Texas.

Arizona Coral Snake lives in rocky areas in southern Arizona and New Mexico. Harmless **Milk Snakes** and **Scarlet Snake** have bands of color in which red and yellow do not touch.

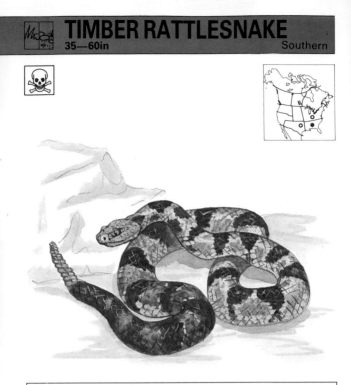

Southern forms are yellow-gray or gray-brown with wavy crossbands and a red-brown stripe on the back. Northern forms are generally darker with dark blotches, and crossbands at rear of body. Both forms have dark tail with rattle at end.

Gathers in large groups in and near dens in wooded areas on south-facing exposures for much of the year, except in summer. Retreats if allowed, but rattles and then strikes if cornered. Venom deadly. Feeds on small mammals, amphibians and birds.

Found mostly in mountain areas, on hillsides, ledges and rocky woodland in north, in wilderness thickets and swamps in south, mostly exterminated elsewhere. Most of eastern USA except Great Lakes region and Maine. Only rattlesnake in northeast.

Massasauga may be dark like some Timber Rattlesnakes, but has nine large scales on top of head.

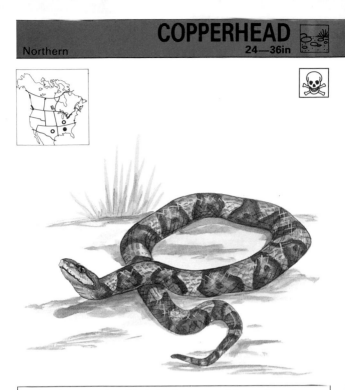

A light brown snake with darker brown or red-brown hourglass-shaped blotches on its back, and a reddish head without markings. Possesses facial pits, one on each side of the head between eye and nostril.

Active by day but nocturnal in hot weather. Hides under log piles and leaves or basks on rocks. Retreats if allowed but strikes if approached too closely; venom rarely fatal if first aid is prompt. Feeds on small mammals, lizards and amphibians.

Found in dry woodland, often in rocky upland areas, but in lowland areas in summer. In southern USA from Massachusetts south to Georgia, west as far as Kansas and Texas.

Four subspecies varying in range, color and pattern. Harmless **Milk Snakes** have wide bands with square marks on underside, not hourglass-shaped blotches.

117

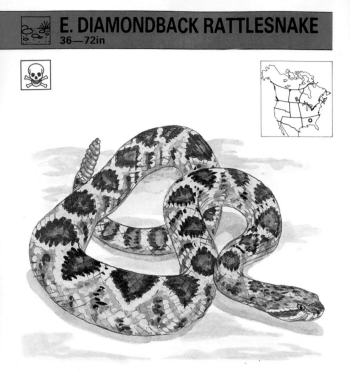

The largest rattlesnake. A thick-bodied gray-green snake with dark diamond-shaped blotches, edged with cream-colored scales and with gray-green centers. There are distinct light lines on the sides of the head.

May hide in Gopher Tortoise burrows. Aggressive, rattling while an enemy is some distance away. Very dangerous with deadly venom, especially if taken by surprise and given no time to rattle. Feeds on rabbits and other small mammals.

Found in dry areas like wooded hillsides, pine and oak woods and farmlands in the coastal plain of southeastern USA from N. Carolina to Mississippi.

Timber Rattlesnake has pattern of wavy lines, not cream-edged diamonds.

W. DIAMONDBACK RATTLESNAKE
30—70in

A heavy snake, the largest of the western rattlesnakes. Gray or light brown in color with darker spots, and a row of light-bordered hexagonal blotches along the back. Tail has black and white rings.

Mostly active in late afternoon and at night. Aggressive and dangerous and will stand its ground, rattling and then striking at an enemy from a coiled position. Venom deadly. Feeds on small mammals, lizards and birds.

Found in arid and semi-arid areas, dry prairies, deserts and foothills usually in brush. Southwestern USA from southeast Calif. to Texas, Oklahoma and Arkansas.

Smaller **Western Rattler** has pattern of blotches at front, crossbands at rear; tail has no black and white rings. Other western rattlesnakes have restricted distributions.

Index and check-list

All species in roman type are illustrated
Keep a record of your sightings by checking the boxes